SpringerBriefs in Applied Sciences and Technology

PoliMI SpringerBriefs

Editorial Board

Barbara Pernici, Politecnico di Milano, Milano, Italy
Stefano Della Torre, Politecnico di Milano, Milano, Italy
Bianca M. Colosimo, Politecnico di Milano, Milano, Italy
Tiziano Faravelli, Politecnico di Milano, Milano, Italy
Roberto Paolucci, Politecnico di Milano, Milano, Italy
Silvia Piardi, Politecnico di Milano, Milano, Italy

More information about this series at http://www.springer.com/series/11159
http://www.polimi.it

Grazia Concilio · Ilaria Tosoni
Editors

Innovation Capacity and the City

The Enabling Role of Design

Editors
Grazia Concilio
DASTU
Politecnico di Milano
Milan, Italy

Ilaria Tosoni
DASTU
Politecnico di Milano
Milan, Italy

ISSN 2191-530X　　　　　　ISSN 2191-5318　(electronic)
SpringerBriefs in Applied Sciences and Technology
ISSN 2282-2577　　　　　　ISSN 2282-2585　(electronic)
PoliMI SpringerBriefs
ISBN 978-3-030-00122-3　　　ISBN 978-3-030-00123-0　(eBook)
https://doi.org/10.1007/978-3-030-00123-0

Library of Congress Control Number: 2018954858

© The Editor(s) (if applicable) and The Author(s) 2019. This book is an open access publication.
Open Access This book is licensed under the terms of the Creative Commons Attribution 4.0 International License (http://creativecommons.org/licenses/by/4.0/), which permits use, sharing, adaptation, distribution and reproduction in any medium or format, as long as you give appropriate credit to the original author(s) and the source, provide a link to the Creative Commons license and indicate if changes were made.
The images or other third party material in this book are included in the book's Creative Commons license, unless indicated otherwise in a credit line to the material. If material is not included in the book's Creative Commons license and your intended use is not permitted by statutory regulation or exceeds the permitted use, you will need to obtain permission directly from the copyright holder.
The use of general descriptive names, registered names, trademarks, service marks, etc. in this publication does not imply, even in the absence of a specific statement, that such names are exempt from the relevant protective laws and regulations and therefore free for general use.
The publisher, the authors and the editors are safe to assume that the advice and information in this book are believed to be true and accurate at the date of publication. Neither the publisher nor the authors or the editors give a warranty, express or implied, with respect to the material contained herein or for any errors or omissions that may have been made. The publisher remains neutral with regard to jurisdictional claims in published maps and institutional affiliations.

This Springer imprint is published by the registered company Springer Nature Switzerland AG
The registered company address is: Gewerbestrasse 11, 6330 Cham, Switzerland

Foreword

This book makes up one of the key milestones of the DESIGNSCAPES project, an H2020 CSA (Coordination and Support Action) funded by the European Commission under the Call entitled "User-driven innovation: value creation through Design Enabled Innovation". The Action started in June 2017 and currently involves 12 public and private organizations (mostly academia and local government associations, plus an international news aggregator) from 10 EU Member States, under the leadership of ANCI Toscana, the free association of Tuscan Municipalities.

The project, as is clear from its full title, aims to build a European capability for Design Enabled Innovation (henceforth: DEI) within the public as well as the private sector, thus meeting a precise requirement of the H2020 Call. However, it does so by taking a relatively unexplored (by previous researchers and practitioners) perspective. In fact, available evidence from both scientific and grey literature highlights the role and importance of design and design thinking for urban development processes, or puts emphasis on the City as testbed or 'lighthouse' of smart technological and social innovation. To this evidence, DESIGNSCAPES adds an original analysis of the visible and hidden connections between the urban context, or 'scape', in which public and private organizations are embedded, and their propensity and capabilities to use design effectively when innovating products, processes and methods of work.

This book is the result of the first 6 months of such analysis and is, therefore, to be considered as a work in progress—although most of the content that will follow does already demonstrate sufficient robustness, at least from a scientific point of view, to appear convincing and encouraging to the policy-oriented reader, until any contrary evidence is found out.

In addition, the main research avenues presented herein are influencing and shaping the imminent launch of yet another exciting initiative of our Action: a funded call for pilot proposals, which will be open to any individual, private or public body, in order to demonstrate adherence to the H2020 Call plea for more extended DEI take-up, while at the same time revealing some of the less obvious 'plots' documenting the connection between the 'Urbanscape' and the intensity or quality or efficiency of that take-up.

Here, at ANCI Toscana, we are proud to be leading such an endeavour; however, we are also aware that the authors of this book are responsible for having first conceived, and then raising to a significant level of clarity and depth in terms of their communication, the building blocks of the theory and some of their practical implications, to be tested and enriched during the pilot phase.

This said, I hope you will enjoy reading the book as much as I did.

Firenze, Italy
Simone Gheri
ANCI Toscana
Director

Acknowledgements

With this publication, the requirements are fulfilled for Deliverable 1.1 of the DESIGNSCAPES project, an H2020 Coordination and Support Action funded by the European Commission. However, the opinions expressed herein are solely of the authors and do not reflect the official standpoints of any EU institution.

Individual contributions of the aforementioned authors have been highlighted by including them in the authors list at the beginning of each book chapter, lead authors are identified by using an envelope symbol within parenthesis. This does not do full justice, however, to the co-creation process that has led to the key original concepts described in this Introduction, which has taken place through several meetings and the exchange of early drafts between the months of August and December 2017. Since then, the Politecnico di Milano as well as ANCI Toscana have taken up the editorial role, bringing the final assembly of chapters to the dignity of a refereed book.

Every possible care has been taken for the removal of any typo and the clarification of the key terms and concepts developed in this publication, including the accompanying references where relevant. However, the authors remain solely responsible for any mistake and apologize in advance for any inconvenience involuntarily caused.

Book editors are grateful to all the DESIGNSCAPES partners and authors of the chapters. A special thank goes to Talita Medina Amaral for the precious support infinalizing the book's pictures and to Carolina Pacchi for reading the draft and providing precious feedbacks.

Contents

1. **Introduction** 1
   Grazia Concilio and Ilaria Tosoni

2. **A Triplet Under Focus: Innovation, Design and the City** 15
   Munir Abbasi, Joe Cullen, Chuan Li, Francesco Molinari,
   Nicola Morelli, Pau Rausell, Luca Simeone, Lampros Stergioulas,
   Ilaria Tosoni and Kirsten Van Dam

3. **Cities as Enablers of Innovation** 43
   Grazia Concilio, Chuan Li, Pau Rausell and Ilaria Tosoni

4. **Innovation and Design** 61
   Grazia Concilio, Amalia De Götzen, Francesco Molinari,
   Nicola Morelli, Ingrid Mulder, Luca Simeone, Ilaria Tosoni
   and Kirsten Van Dam

5. **Design Enabled Innovation in Urban Environments** 85
   Grazia Concilio, Joe Cullen and Ilaria Tosoni

Chapter 1
Introduction

Grazia Concilio and Ilaria Tosoni

1.1 Cities as Breeding Grounds: What Answers to Global Challenges?

It is unquestionable that the global community is challenged by distressing crises (political, social, economic and environmental), which are sometimes referred to as "wicked problems" due to their idiosyncratic, and apparently impossible to tackle, nature. These problems often display a huge interconnectedness (they are reciprocally reinforcing) and may be generative of new issues (a sort of challenge-within-the-challenge mechanism), making their proper handling even harder and any adopted approach highly controversial. These crises are recurrent and similar from place to place, but their magnitude is growing in size and affecting people on a global scale, thus making the task of approaching them far too complex for any single stakeholder or territorial community alone. For these reasons, now more than ever, new individual behaviours and collective practices, innovative rules and norms, novel local and national policies and wider international cooperation agreements often occur and are widely experimented on, all over the world, bringing about sustainable solutions at multiple levels and scales.

Cities are directly affected by most of these crises and, at the same time, represent the place where the larger sustainability game is played. However, as most people think, the overwhelming challenges embedded in city life for individuals, families, civil societies and governments can, and must, be seen also as opportunities for innovation, diffused equity, more diligent foresight and, above all, pragmatism. In fact, it is not only due to the urbanization trends that we turn to cities when we look for solutions to the wicked problems that the world faces. Free from national and global politics, though always acting in its shadow, cities are,

---

G. Concilio (✉) · I. Tosoni
Dipartimento di Architettura e Studi Urbani, Politecnico di Milano, Milan, Italy
e-mail: grazia.concilio@polimi.it

© The Author(s) 2019
G. Concilio and I. Tosoni (eds.), *Innovation Capacity and the City*,
PoliMI SpringerBriefs, https://doi.org/10.1007/978-3-030-00123-0_1

more and more, places where creative problem-solving flourishes (sometimes out of necessity, sometimes by purposeful construct) even when such issues as climate change, migration, and economic inequality are at the forefront of change makers. Cities know how to get things done, and they are doing just that all over the world (Brescia and Marshall 2016a).

Further to the above, cities provide crucial resources for our future (Brescia and Marshall 2016a). This is because they are not simply population aggregation centres: they are knowledge hubs and sustainable power plants; they serve as first shelters for immigrant people; they are fertile environments for old and new trading and innovation projects (Brescia and Marshall 2016b). It is hence there that intelligent, local answers to global challenges can be and are being identified and experimented.

For a long time, however, cities have been seen as passive participants to multilateral efforts for a more sustainable development. Now, it is clear and globally shared that they are key actors in this global and planetary battle: they are asked increasingly often to take charge of the necessary, often complex, transitions.

To this end, however, cities must become fully aware of being key environments for change, due to the huge density of resources, energies, knowledge and skills within (Dvir and Pasher 2004) and also due to their interconnected nature, which enables place-based interactions to materialize among different operators, organizations, initiatives, institutions, etc. In these systems of an urban nature, one finds the right breeding ground to stimulate the emergence or integration of innovative solutions, capable of contributing to ignite the necessary and urgent systemic changes and transitions in local and global communities.

However, envisioning, designing and governing transformations, while working in such complex environments, requires an intense dialogue between different, and sometimes distant, disciplines and practices, theories and applications, cultures and visions, acting as co-located forces, i.e. all being active in a same place.

In addition, capturing, designing, guiding and spreading out those transformations which can be relevant for the global challenges is also complex work, which requires aligning and synergizing differences and uniformities, immutability and instability, continuity and discontinuity. This work must also be carried out within environments that are often as complex as the problems themselves.

Within every city to some extent, this acknowledgment and instrumentalisation of transformations can effectively begin, as it is there that the networked nature of the individuals and resources involved can find accessible hubs to access the dynamic and creative flows of the necessary information, knowledge and practices. Yet, cities are not alike when it comes to triggering, generating, hosting, and scaling up systemic and sustainable change (Molinari and Concilio 2016). Indeed, they show very diverse political, infrastructural, organizational and societal conditions, which act in different ways to preserve the status quo or foster new value creation, to prevent or facilitate innovation and to impede or ensure that it has a broader impact (Puerari et al. 2017). Overall, these conditions can be said to belong to two main and distinct groups (Puerari 2016). The first group is related to the productivity and vitality of a city's cultural environment, including:

- Presence of physical spaces and opportunities for experimenting and learning (Concilio 2016; Karvonen and van Heur 2014; Nonaka et al. 2000);
- Density, diversity and richness of the experiments already taking place therein (Asheim and Coenen 2007; Rotmans and Loorbach 2009);
- Emergence of creative communities who co-design and incubate new, innovative initiatives (Meroni and Sangiorgi 2011).

The second group of conditions refers to the institutional capacity and infrastructure of a city, notably:

- Existence of *ad hoc* policy frameworks, such as norms, contracts and informal agreements, which allow both experimentation and stabilization of certain improvements (Chesbrough et al. 2006; Murray et al. 2010; Puerari 2016);
- Institutional and business ability to capture and align existing innovation "niches" that might be relevant for systemic change (Geels 2011; Puerari et al. 2013);
- Availability of specific strategies for activating or hosting innovation (Huxham and Vangen 2000; Marsh et al. 2013);
- Existence of creative and suggestive places whereby innovative solutions to public problems are developed through the creation of networks, partnerships and events (Manzini 2015).

The various possible combinations of these characteristics give rise to a wide, rich and diversified scenario of global cities that differ from each other in terms of how they organize themselves, aggregate existing resources and respond to the challenges they are ready, able, or sensitive enough to explore, experiment on and deal with (Puerari et al. 2017).

1.2 How Can We Accompany Transition Processes?

Innovation is considered to be the panacea shelter under which responses to the planetary struggle must be identified and through which urban societies can accomplish their difficult and complex tasks; this is asserted at any level, by expert observers as well as local, regional, national and international authorities; this is the main target of any agency or actor, public or private; this appears crucial at any scale. "Innovation is the answer" and everyone needs to look for it, make it real and achieve it in any domain and action sphere.

Considering the breadth and relevance of the problems at hand, however, any innovation process needs to be framed in terms of the wider impacts targeted, determining the level at which innovation itself is engaged in the sustainability game. The search for radical, game-changing and at the same time sustainable tools, solutions and ideas is widespread all over the globe and mobilizes both researchers and practitioners to look for new answers inside the dominant, market-centred growth model, as well as those looking for universally original "new economic models". The latter range across very diverse thoughts: from models of low- or no-growth, to various qualitative and quantitative models of the post-growth and de-growth literature (Castells et al. 2017).

We share with den Ouden (2012) the idea that building innovations responding to societal challenges requires us to consider a large number of aspects at the same time; this usually crosses the borders of a single decision maker's skill set, or individual discipline, organization or community. In fact, imagining, creating and developing these innovations requires the simultaneous consideration of different perspectives: of the user who may potentially adopt the new solution, of the organisation that will convey the product/service to the market, of the marketplace/ecosystem that will link the various products and services to their users and other stakeholders, and finally of the entire society, which will take benefit from the established solution.

Although such problems appear to be insoluble, the global challenges provide tremendous opportunities for innovators targeting shared values (Porter and Kramer 2011). Now more than ever, innovators can find collaborative allies in policy makers dealing with urban crises, leading to a situation where profit is only one possible outcome of a specific innovation, which is often instrumental to a wider set of aims than mere monetary success.

But there is more. According to den Ouden (2012), this is a prosperous moment for a growing and widespread sense of awareness with regards to the political, societal, economic and environmental issues we face. Such awareness is creating favourable conditions for a mass adoption of the solutions providing clear answers to those issues. In turn, this trend is bringing us out of the era of knowledge economy (Powell and Snellman 2004) towards the era of transformative economy (Mermiri 2009; den Ouden 2012; Megens et al. 2013). In this new situation, innovation is asked to address global challenges and at the same time deliver solutions that people would love to use, which also ensures a greater market success to related products and services. The transformative economy generates solutions to the big collective issues giving priority the collective rather than the individual interests and needs, thus leading to a mass, rather than limited, change in behaviour (Megens et al. 2013).

Indeed, transformation takes place

> At societal level, through large numbers of individuals willingly contributing to it (…); global challenges are guiding and aligning intentions and availabilities of world citizens as never before and this is making more and more the intended transformation possible. This current alignment represents a great opportunity for the market to use it for the targeted business and for the benefit of the global society at the same time (den Ouden 2012: 9).

In other words, the two impacts—societal and business—coexist and reciprocally influence each other, as also witnessed by a plethora of innovative initiatives around the world that are entirely and exclusively committed to sustainability, equity and on solving global challenges as well as being rather indifferent to the goals of economic growth and market success.

According to Castells et al. (2017), however, this new way of reasoning is not enough to produce the proclaimed results; it is only yet another attempt of a persistent capitalist culture and economic and market-based model to survive cyclical crises with formal set-ups. In the very end, what we can expect is that the goal of succeeding in the market will always prevail over the ambition to provide effective societal problem solving. A radically different perspective would therefore be needed, which starts to look at innovations, especially those driven by the business community, as irredeemably weak and ineffective with respect to the changes required by the global scenario.

Indeed, these authors believe that the only effective responses to global challenges can come from solutions that are sensitive to the bigger issues but also narrowly focused on the innovators' potential for revenue, solutions that are inspired and at the same time enabled by the necessity to survive on a daily basis, thus guaranteeing a broader and more democratic access to future opportunities—in brief, solutions that explore and put new and disruptive economic models to the test, finding workable answers for the many rather than the few.

This alternative perspective is nowadays supported, according to Castells et al. (2017), by a global team of researchers including not only environmental, institutional, or political economists, but also geographers, ecologists and sociologists. Indeed, their working agenda is transdisciplinary and not at all oriented to introduce new mathematics or statistics as theoretical foundations, but to give birth to an entirely "new economic model", grounded on the emergent micro practices that are already challenging the dominant capitalistic logic: driven by sharing economic principles, using virtual currencies or local monies, leading to subsidiarity in action and not only in concept, etc.

We can see two normative—if not ideological—visions facing one another here.

The supporters of the first vision believe that innovative solutions responding to global challenges are hardly successful when disruptive, or have more chances of surviving if only incremental. This is due to the need for any sustainable innovation to overcome two big obstacles: the first refers to the resistance that the dominant culture or the prevailing economic model put in place against any attempt at challenging their basic principles and mechanisms; the second obstacle refers to the hard and diffused changes in users' or citizens' behaviour that many disruptive solutions demand to scale up and ultimately be adopted. In this view, the effectiveness of an innovation in responding to global challenges is highest when the value of the solution is clearly recognized by a majority of people, so that its adoption does not require too complicated changes and, consequently, the new behaviours and practices can be more easily spread and scaled up.

The supporters of the second vision take the opposite stance: global challenges can only be faced by innovative solutions emerging outside the dominant market economy culture, thus being disruptive by definition, as well as supportive of a wholly reversed view of the world. Community or sharing economies, street level initiatives, local currencies, grassroot innovations: all these and other examples somehow challenge the existing model, although some researchers may consider them only as refurnishing approaches and not real alternatives to the market-based model. These are the outputs of either a voluntary search for a paradigm shift or insurgent energies looking for solutions to local, small scale problems which are unchallenged by the market; they often do not have the ability to scale up singularly but their diffusion is phenomenally growing (Concilio and Molinari 2015) and the global scenario displays a complex and diversified geography of very similar looking cases.

To sum up, innovation forces are not entirely and homogenously committed to a single way to deal with global challenges; however, available experiences increasingly converge towards societal aims and this makes them perfectly aligned with a transitioning and problem-solving approach. In any case, cities play a crucial role in innovation: they may act as testbed environments for new solutions to be commercially exploited at a later stage, in accordance with the first vision; or they may be the cradles of emerging practices, suggesting alternative ways to grow and challenge the market-based model, as suggested by the second vision.

1.3 What Role Can Design Play?

Whatever vision one adheres to when dealing with global challenges through local innovation, the need to activate values and meanings that are crucial for the transition processes is unquestionable. For us, this is the main role design should play.

Design is not a new profession and is traditionally related to "creative problem-solving", whereas it is clear that conventional problem-solving is not effective or powerful enough. As a creative problem-solving ability, i.e. capable of mobilizing meanings and values (Verganti 2009; den Ouden 2012), design appears to be the way to achieve societal transformation by localizing change (making a transition concrete), questioning it (reflecting on its quality), and opening it up (expanding its sense) (Sennett 2008).

Remaining loyal to the distinction introduced by Buchanan (1992, 1995, 1998) as quoted by Scupelli (2015), four orders of design can be identified: "first order as symbolic and visual communication (signs and symbols), usually understood as communication design; second order as material objects, usually understood as the realm of industrial product design; third order as activities and services, usually understood as service design and logistics; and the fourth order as complex systems and environments for living, working, playing, and learning, usually understood as systems engineering, architecture, and urban planning" (Scupelli 2015: 80).

To contribute to transition, design outputs, effects and impacts should intersect the four orders above. Scupelli considers that to be a consequence of a design intention, which he calls "transition design"[1]; still it is evident that other design

---

[1]Transition Design is an area of design research, practice and study that was conceived at the School of Design at Carnegie Mellon University in 2012 and integrated into new programs and curricula launched in Fall 2014. More at: https://design.cmu.edu/sites/default/files/Transition_Design_Monograph_final.pdf (last accessed: December 2017).

intentions, maybe less strategic and less aware of the different orders and levels of change needed for transition, can achieve similar results. In this latter case, however, a certain design ability is still necessary in order to capture these achievements and connect them to—or value them for—the complex phenomena involved in transition. This in turn obviously integrates several trajectories of change, all being driven by a more or less aware and forward-looking design intention. A significant aspect here is the strong emphasis given by a common use of binomials such as design and transition (Scupelli 2015), design and sustainability (Manzini 2007; Crocker and Lehmann 2013), design and systemic changes (Brown 2009), all revealing a shared view among researchers of design being fundamental to drive, support, enable and value the specific innovations needed to tackle global challenges.

Design-for is thus widening its importance with respect to *design-of* and this further expands the expectations towards design: no longer only a way to produce innovation, but in many respects a key approach to embedding innovation in complex socio-technical contexts, "the" way to work effectively in the perspective of transitioning.

Policy design, design for better governance of innovation processes, design for supporting innovation ecosystems: these concepts reveal a theoretical and practical shift that makes it extremely promising to introduce an additional binomial: city and design.

Cities are in fact very stimulating and productive environments for design: not only are they arenas for global crises, they are also places where transition opportunities emerge and mature with the highest density, hence innovations need to be aligned and synergized towards transition. Thus, design can be considered the way for innovation processes to be embedded within cities; cities, on the other hand, can prove to be rich and proactive hosts wherein design processes can effectively be adopted.

1.4 About This Book

Adopting design as a way to embed innovation within urban environments, in order to conceptualize feasible answers to complex global challenges, is the core topic of this book. In particular, our line of reasoning tries to reduce the conflict between those innovators who, despite targeting societal change and sustainability, adhere to the classical economic model and therefore look for market success and profitability and those who, otherwise and in opposition to such mindsets, do not focus on the potential for revenue from their innovations and promote alternative ideas and economies. To that end, this book explores the conditions for innovation to be disruptive of values yet, at the same time, gradual during the dynamics of change. For us, disruptiveness, with regards to values, is the best guarantee for establishing an effective path to sustainability, while the gradual aspect is crucial to reduce the risk of a dull resistance of the predominant socio-economic system.

With such an intent in mind, the book puts together three key concept domains rarely considered in a unitary fashion. They are: *innovation*, the only possible response to global crises, aiming at transforming behaviours and practices towards systemic changes and transition; *design*, a way of creatively conceiving, developing and driving forward new practices for undertaking large scale transitions; and *cities*, seen as the environments where problems present themselves in the most socially relevant way and at the same time as key opportunities for testing and adopting forms of innovation which target global challenges.

Therefore, given the setup and aims of our reasoning, we interrogate how the interplay between design and the urban dimension can contribute to sparking or fastening the various pathways of the innovation process. The book discusses these issues moving from some key research hypotheses.

H1. The application of design approaches and tools can facilitate the generation of innovations in urban contexts both as an endogenous process relating to local resources and as a result of embedding innovations from other contexts with similar, or even dissimilar conditions.

H2. The application of design approaches and tools may help propagate local innovation skills and capacities within urban contexts not having previously been exposed, to the required extent, to other innovation facilitating conditions.

H3. The application of design approaches and tools can facilitate the scaling, embedding and/or transferring, of innovations born from some urban contexts into other contexts having similar, or even dissimilar conditions.

Operationally, what we will be looking at are multiple (sub)processes, including:

- The dynamics of innovation pathways and their interactions with the urban dimensions and resources;
- The skill and capacity building processes, enabled by design, leading to those relevant dynamics;
- The creation of the conditions for scaling innovation in a generative dialogue with the city;
- The creation of the conditions for distributing innovations "born elsewhere" and the generation of local "hubs" of actors dealing specifically with such innovations, and/or the transformation of those innovations into something else, more tailored to the local situation, or even dramatically different.

The last point alludes to Jacobs' belief in a powerful multiplier effect of the "two interlocking reciprocating systems" leading to "explosive city growth".

As per our second caveat, we do not intend to follow such a line of thought to the point of considering a massive take up and a diffused emergence of innovations as the inevitable outcome of adding design tools, methods and instruments to a supposedly non-design-enabled process. More modestly, we will be satisfied if an "appropriate" injection of those methods and tools, combined with critical awareness for the role of urban dimensions and networks, will "increase" the creative capacity and/or encourage the relevant innovation to be judiciously adopted and put into practice in a certain community or environment.

The book chapters follow this reasoning starting from the exploration of key concepts and then introducing the main research findings.

Chapter 2 positions the three key concepts of cities, design and innovation, as introduced above, in relation to the most relevant academic references. It unfolds them by affirming that a new stance towards innovation is needed. As already argued, innovation (be it technical, societal, institutional, etc.) is essential to tackling the global crises of today (climate change, social exclusion, inequality, food distribution, mass migrations…) which are generated or reinforced by the persistence of systemic ("wicked") problems. The chapter hence explores several definitions of innovation, which are presented and discussed in order to identify the main features of related processes. In the authors' perspective, innovation should be considered as a complex and dynamic multi-phase and multi-level process. The conceptual framework provided by Geels (2002), Grin et al. (2010) describes it as the interplay of transition patterns running at three distinct levels: innovative practices (niche experiments), structure (the so-called regime), and long-term, exogenous trends (the landscape). The conception of a heterogeneous and multi-dimensional process (Grin et al. 2010) brings the reasoning to look at innovation no longer in terms of phases of a linear process, but of stages of maturity in relation to the different patterns of transition. A key finding of the chapter is the conclusion that, in this perspective, there is no use in opposing radical and incremental innovation: different types of innovation need to act at the same time in order to enable successful change to occur (Cruickshank 2014).

Creativity is another key element of innovation that is explored by this book. Usually creativity is associated with specific people and skills, still some authors consider creativity as a relevant human capacity, which is inspired and magnified by plural and multifaceted environments where it is considered a sort of "phenomenon of the multitude", embedded in diversity and interactive behaviours. Here rests the link between (this new way of looking at) innovation and design, the second key concept explored in Chap. 3. As for innovation, in fact, the initial point of view regarding design has shifted from a traditional focus from products to services and then to the design of product-service systems, combining both tangible and intangible elements. Methods, tools and approaches have changed accordingly, gradually moving towards a greater user involvement in the creative process; the chapter offers an overview of the most relevant achievements, focusing on their interaction with the components of innovation processes.

By stressing on non-expert, creative and design competencies, the chapter draws the reader's attention to socio-technical innovation processes. In this perspective, the urban dimension emerges as a key third factor in the process. Cities are cultural, social, economic and spatial entities interacting and participating in innovation processes with their own resources. Specifically, the chapter emphasizes the importance of social learning and the activation of networks in innovation processes and proposes an alternative policy perspective in line with this view.

Chapter 3 explores the interplay between innovation processes and the urban dimension. Cities are considered key environments for the emergence of generative interactions and innovation networks. Cities are therefore scanned thoroughly in order to sense all potential cues for their ability to set the innovation cycles in motion. Furthermore, the relationship between cities and innovation in present times can also be regarded from a different perspective. As it is vital to rethink our development patterns, in order to contrast global warming and its ominous threats, cities are themselves concrete materials for innovation. As they are areas where problems related to unsustainable consumption of non-recoverable resources (soil, energy, water, food, …) assume a critical dimension in terms of actual liveability—not to speak of traffic congestion, air pollution, migration, social exclusion etc.—cities challenge the very same concept of innovation by adding a feature of long-term positive effects to its social assessment framework. The city is therefore seen both as a hotbed of creativity and innovative culture and a place where different actors (policy makers, civil servants, NGOs, citizens, start-uppers, entrepreneurs, etc.) receive continuous stimuli to engage in innovations that fulfil specific needs (be they market, organisational or community related).

The chapter then focuses on the distinctive elements of what is urban, which can be considered relevant in the development processes of new ideas, products, services, etc. Each city presents a specific combination of those layers of attributes, which ultimately describe its unique identity and potential capability of establishing the conditions for creative innovation processes to be embedded. The chapter then analyses five features considered the most significant in relation to Design Enabled Innovation (DEI): 1. The City as a marketplace; 2. The City as a problems lab; 3. The City as an idearium; 4. The City as a resource pot; and 5. The City as a political arena. These five dimensions can be defined as "interfaces" through which a city interacts with innovation processes. Those processes in turn vary significantly, depending on the innovation's stage of maturity and the way in which innovation processes enter the city through its networks.

Alongside interfaces, which intercept innovation processes at an operational level, another key concept introduced by the book is that of "Urbanscape". The Urbanscape is described as the set of conditions making a city a prone or adverse environment towards innovation and innovation networks. The five components of the Urbanscape are presented and discussed.

Chapter 4 focuses on the relationship between innovation and design. It therefore acknowledges how the focus of design studies has shifted from a product-centric perspective to a perspective that is centred on the interaction between the consumer and service context (so called Service Dominant Logic), in which value is defined by and co-created with the consumer, rather than embedded in the output (Vargo and Lusch 2004: 6). The fundamental change in this approach is illustrated by Vargo and Lusch's statement that the enterprise cannot deliver value, but only offer value propositions, which means that it cannot create or deliver value independently (Vargo and Lusch 2008). The chapter then elaborates on the key aspects of these processes of co-production of value as the result of a myriad of activities performed by many people dispersed in time and space. A definition of design is then proposed, as the process through which possibilities are consciously created (Metcalf 2014: vii).

The reasoning then goes on by identifying two distinct design competencies and agencies: diffuse and expert. Diffuse design is meant as a "natural capacity" (Manzini 2015: 47) that is largely distributed and widely applied to frame and solve everyday problems and, more generally, to make sense of things (Manzini 2015; Krippendorff 2006; Schön 1987). On the other hand, while diffuse design is a general human capacity and activity, some people study and practice design at an expert level. Furthermore, design processes might not only be driven by human agencies (e.g., diffuse or expert design), but can also be affected by other agencies, i.e. socio-technical, institutional or cultural factors. Both diffuse and expert design work as enablers at different stages of the change process and different levels of the socio-technical structures—from localized and context-anchored projects to projects that specifically frame the embedding of the design product into the social and political realm; staying within Geels' (2002, 2011) framework, we can say that they act either in niches or in regimes.

Another key concept introduced in Chap. 5 is that of "infrastructuring". The term describes the expert design intervention in resource aggregation and therefore value-creation. It describes how an expert designer can support diffuse design by triggering, inspiring or facilitating people's creativity, or engaging with them in value-co-creation. Infrastructuring hence includes the most common design activities, consisting in aggregating technical knowledge, professional experience, existing tools and technologies, to generate products and services which users will use to produce value that addresses their own needs.

The reasoning then focuses on the interplay between innovation processes and design. Moving from Verganti's (2009) conceptualization of design-driven innovation, the attempt is to define the space of interaction between the different components of the innovation process. Specifically, by adding the contribution of design in its two defined agencies (diffuse and expert) we can define a 3D space where deeply different innovation practices and experiences are to be located. In this way we can also try to cluster and name them while revealing the mechanisms and factors affecting the quality of innovation outputs. This exercise effectively empowers the book's initial hypothesis: no innovation is possible without design.

In Chap. 5 we explore the dynamics of change in urban systems. Embedment is a key concept to understand those processes, which unfold mainly as co-evolution processes involving innovations development, use and adoption, their mutual adaptation and ultimate adjustment to institutional, organisational, regulative, social and practical contexts (Grin et al. 2010: 11). We are therefore observing spatialized learning processes: the spaces through which knowledge moves are not simply landscapes of learning, but constitutive of it. In urban spaces, learning produced by innovation operates as a form of 'education of attention' (Gibson 1969; Ingold 2000), a socio-political rooting of new values (activated by large scale creation of new value meanings and functions). This means that spatialized learning happens through intensive, haptic immersion, based on three key actions: "translation", "coordination" and "dwelling" (McFarlane 2011). Translation is defined as the relational distribution through which learning is produced as a socio-material epistemology of displacement and change; coordination refers to the construction of functional systems that enable learning as a means of coping with complexity and facilitating adaptation; lastly dwelling is regarded as a process of education of attention through which learning operates as a way of seeing and inhabiting urban worlds (McFarlane 2011).

Learning dynamics are the way innovation is ignited, at a very early stage of maturity, in a specific urban environment by contributing to, or being inspired by, the *urban interfaces* as described in Chap. 4. Relevant for innovation to capture the offered potentials is therefore the capacity to activate new connections with such forces while disconnecting others, i.e. to activate new modes for knowledge and value creation through the interaction with the provided interfaces. It is in these dynamics that design approaches can play at best their enabling role. Design can be seen as a social integrator and the enabler of the learning dynamics depicted above. In our perspective, design enables the possibility for solutions (at any innovation maturity stage) to be embedded within specific urban contexts and is able to develop and work with these solutions in order for to be relevant in other contexts. This act of embedding represents a (design) endeavour situated between meaning and function (see the 3D model), which shapes value by infrastructuring practices in real life, which are targeted by the innovation process.

Design Enabled Innovation in urban environments is therefore a non-linear, multi-causal, multilevel and networked process of change aimed at producing new functions, uses and meanings while empowering values derived from a shared view of key issues/challenges enabled by the action of design skills and approaches. In this perspective, creative processes create a dialogue with complexity-generating innovative solutions to urban problems. The urban thus produces DEI primarily in two ways: the city guarantees the existence of conditions (normative, economic, cognitive, informational and networking) for the activation of Design Enabled Innovation processes; however it also inspires ideas because it is the city that faces most of today's global challenges. Urban problems and challenges tend to nest in the *complexity zone* (Stacey 2002); therefore, they call for creative solutions developed through erratic (i.e. less structured and open) decision making.

The chapter then introduces a reflection on key features to sense innovation in urban environments as a way for policy makers, designers and firms to intercept innovation niches and processes in their context.

References

Asheim BT, Coenen LVJ (2007) Face-to-face, buzz and knowledge bases: socio-spatial implications for learning, innovation and innovation policy. Environ Plann C Gov Policy 25:655–670

Brescia R, Marshall JT (2016a) Preface. In: Brescia R, Marshall JT (eds) How cities will save the world. Routledge, New York

Brescia R, Marshall JT (2016b) Introduction. In: Brescia R, Marshall JT (eds) How cities will save the world. Routledge, New York, pp 1–10

Brown T (2009) Change by design. How design thinking transforms organisations and inspires innovation. Harper Collins e-books

Buchanan R (1992) Wicked problems in design thinking. Des Issues 8(2):5–21

Buchanan R (1995) Rhetoric, humanism, and design. In: Buchanan R, Margolin V, (eds) Discovering design: explorations in design studies. University of Chicago Press

Buchanan R (1998) Branzi's dilemma: design in contemporary culture. Des Issues 14(1):3–20. Spring

Castells M et al (2017) Another economy is possible: culture and economy in a time of crisis. Polity Press, Cambridge

Chesbrough HW, Vanhaverbeke W, West J (2006) Open innovation: researching a new paradigm. Oxford University Press, Oxford

Concilio G (2016) Urban living labs: opportunities in and for planning. In: Rizzo F, Concilio G (eds) Human smart cities. rethinking the interplay between design and planning. Springer, London

Concilio G, Molinari F (2015) Place-based innovation: analysing the "social streets" phenomenon. In: Proceedings of the IFKAD 2015 conference, pp 10–12, June, Bari

Crocker R, Lehmann S (eds) (2013) Motivating change: sustainable design and behaviour in the built environment. Earthscan Publishing for a Sustainable Future, London

Cruickshank L (2014) New design processes for knowledge exchange tools for the new IDEAS project. In: Paper presented at the creative exchange conference, Lancaster, United Kingdom. Design Council UK

den Ouden E (2012) Innovation design. Creating value for people, organisations and society. Springer-Verlag, London

Dvir R, Pasher E (2004) Innovation engines for knowledge cities: an innovation ecology perspective. J Knowl Manag 8(5):16–27

Geels FW (2002) Technological transitions as evolutionary reconfiguration processes: a multi-level perspective and a case-study. Res Policy 31:8–9: 257–1274

Geels FW (2011) The multi-level perspective on sustainability transitions: responses to seven criticisms. Env Innov Soc Transit 1(1):24–40

Gibson EJ (1969) Principles of perceptual learning and development. Appleton-Century Crofts, New York

Grin J, Rotmans J, Schot, (2010) Transitions to sustainable development: new directions in the study of long term transformative change. Routledge, New York

Huxham C, Vangen S (2000) What makes partnerships work? In: Osborne SP (ed) Public-private partnerships. Theory and practice in international perspective. Taylor and Francis group, Routledge, pp 293–310

Ingold T (2000) The perception of the environment: essays on livelihood, dwelling and skill. Routledge, London

Karvonen A, van Heur B (2014) Urban laboratories: experiments in reworking cities. Int J Urban Reg Res 38(2):379–392

Krippendorff K (2006) Semantic turn: new foundations for design. CRC, Taylor and Francis, Boca Raton

Manzini E (2007) Design research for sustainable social innovation. In: Michel R (ed) Design research now. Board of International Research in Design. Birkhäuser, Basel

Manzini E (2015) Design, when everybody designs: an introduction to social innovation. MIT Press, Cambridge, London

Marsh J, Molinari F, Trapani F (2013) Co-creating urban development: a living lab for community regeneration in the second district of Palermo. In: Murgante B, Misra S, Carlini M, Torre CM, Nguyen HQ, Taniar D, Gervasi O (eds) Computational science and its applications, ICCSA 2013 Ho Chi Minh City, Vietnam, pp 294–308

McFarlane C (2011) The city as a machine for learning. Trans Insts Br Geogr 36:360–376. https://doi.org/10.1111/j.1475-5661.2011.00430.x

Megens CJPG, Peeters MMR, Funk M, Hummels CCM, Brombacher AC (2013) New craftsmanship in industrial design towards a transformation economy. In: Proceedings of the

10th European academy of design conference: crafting the future, April 17–19, Gothenburg, Sweden
Mermiri T (2009) Beyond experience: culture, consumer & brand, the transformation economy. Arts & Business, London
Meroni A, Sangiorgi D (2011) Design for services. Gower Publishing Ltd, Farnham, Surrey, England
Metcalf GS (2014) Social systems and design. Springer, Japan
Molinari F, Concilio G (2016) Looking for the seeds of scalability. A self-assessment framework for service innovators. In: Proceedings of the ECKM2016 conference, Belfast, UK
Murray R, Caulier-grice J, Mulgan G (2010) The open book of social innovation (Social Inn). The Young Foundation
Nonaka I, Toyama R, Konno N (2000). SECI, Ba and leadership: a unified model of dynamic knowledge creation. Long Range Plann 33(1):5–34
Porter ME, Kramer MR (2011) Creating shared value. How to reinvent capitalism—and unleash a wave of innovation and growth. Harvard Business Review, January–February
Powell WW, Snellman K (2004) The knowledge economy. Ann Rev Sociol 3(August):199–220
Puerari E (2016) Urban public services innovation. Exploring 3P and 4P models. PhD Thesis, Politecnico di Milano
Puerari E, Concilio G, Longo A, Rizzo F (2013). Innovating public services in urban environments: a SOC inspired strategy proposal. In: Schiuma G, Spender J, Public A (eds) Smart growth: organisations, cities and communities. Proceedings of the 8th international forum on knowledge asset dynamics, Zagreb, Croatia, pp 987–1007
Puerari E, De Koning J, Mulder IJ, Loorbach D (2017) Shaping spaces of interaction for sustainable transitions. In: Proceedings of AESOP annual congress. Lisbon, 11–14 July 2017, pp 202–208
Rotmans J, Loorbach DA (2009) Complexity and transition management. J Ind Ecol 13(2):184–196
Schön DA (1987) Educating the reflective practitioner. Jossey-Bass, San Francisco, CA
Scupelli P (2015) Designed transitions and what kind of design is transition design? Des Philos Pap 13(1):75–84
Sennett R (2008) The craftsman. Yale University Press
Stacey RD (2002) Strategic management and organisational dynamics: the challenge of complexity, 3rd edn. Prentice Hall, Harlow
Vargo SL, Lusch R F (2004) Evolving to a new dominant logic for marketing. J Market 68:1–17
Vargo SL, Lusch RF (2008) Service-dominant logic: continuing the evolution. J Acad Mark Sci 36:1–10
Verganti R (2009) Design-driven innovation: changing the rules of competition by radically innovating what things mean. Harvard Business School Publishing, Boston

Open Access This chapter is licensed under the terms of the Creative Commons Attribution 4.0 International License (http://creativecommons.org/licenses/by/4.0/), which permits use, sharing, adaptation, distribution and reproduction in any medium or format, as long as you give appropriate credit to the original author(s) and the source, provide a link to the Creative Commons license and indicate if changes were made.

The images or other third party material in this chapter are included in the chapter's Creative Commons license, unless indicated otherwise in a credit line to the material. If material is not included in the chapter's Creative Commons license and your intended use is not permitted by statutory regulation or exceeds the permitted use, you will need to obtain permission directly from the copyright holder.

Chapter 2
A Triplet Under Focus: Innovation, Design and the City

Munir Abbasi, Joe Cullen, Chuan Li, Francesco Molinari,
Nicola Morelli, Pau Rausell, Luca Simeone, Lampros Stergioulas,
Ilaria Tosoni and Kirsten Van Dam

2.1 The Context of Our Investigation

The role of design in innovation processes is a trendy topic in current debates on business development and competitiveness. Design activities and methods are to be adopted by firms and companies in order to fully exploit their potential and survive in a highly competitive globalized market. There is a great focus on the capability of design processes to integrate business and societal goals in the definition of new products, services, and instruments in response to the great challenges facing the contemporary world. Design has grown in appeal by identifying itself with a series of tools and codified processes and approaches, which manage to face complexity while cultivating an action/solution oriented approach (Scholl 1995). Nevertheless, design and innovation are multifaceted/manifold concepts that need to be explored and understood in their full spectrum: What do we consider innovation? How do innovation processes work? What design approaches better contribute to innovation

---

M. Abbasi · L. Stergioulas
Surrey Business School, University of Surrey, Surrey, UK

J. Cullen
The Tavistock Institute, London, UK

C. Li · P. Rausell
University of Valencia, Valencia, Spain

F. Molinari
ANCI Toscana, Florence, Italy

N. Morelli · L. Simeone · K. Van Dam
Aalborg University, Aalborg, Denmark

I. Tosoni (✉)
Politecnico Di Milano, Milan, Italy
e-mail: ilaria.tosoni@polimi.it

© The Author(s) 2019
G. Concilio and I. Tosoni (eds.), *Innovation Capacity and the City*,
PoliMI SpringerBriefs, https://doi.org/10.1007/978-3-030-00123-0_2

pathways? What is the specific role of design? A disambiguating effort is clearly needed.

A key argument of this book is that, on one hand, a new attitude/approach towards innovation is needed. Innovation (technical, societal, institutional, etc.) is essential to tackling today's global crises (climate change, social exclusion, inequality, food distribution, mass migrations…) generated by the persistence of some systemic problems. The growing social awareness of these issues creates "windows of opportunity" (Grin et al. 2010) to bend the "Market" towards sustainable solutions creating a virtuous synergy between business (firms, capital, …) and societal goals. Firms can learn that there is space for new value propositions (potentially generating revenues) that respond to new demands (values) related to sustainability, environmental awareness, access to resources, etc. On the other hand, the book elaborates on the role of cities as key incubators and laboratories where this kind of innovation can be developed and stress-tested. Design can then be considered the tool which enables us to embed this particular kind of innovation processes into situated production, institutional and social practices and attitudes.

It is therefore relevant and decisive, in order to define a sound interpretative framework, to reason about the urban as the context for adopting Design Enabled Innovation as cities are simultaneously the context where problems are often generated, mostly visible and stratified, while also being the location where opportunities arise from problems when finding their long-term solutions.

The aim of this chapter is therefore to take a position in this debate by defining the three key concepts (innovation, design and the urban dimension) referring to these research domains and theses which best provide a compass with which to navigate towards an operational approach to Design Enabled Innovation in urban environments.

2.2 Positioning Concepts and Definitions

In this section, three main concepts and their components are explored and examined: innovation, design, and cities. Through these concepts, it is further explored in the following chapters how they interact and contribute in a synergic manner to the process of change. The aim of this exploration is to define this book's stance in relation to the debate concerning innovation, its pathways and the manifold factors influencing it. Particularly, as already mentioned, it is important to sharpen our focus on the definitions and interpretations of the three concepts, which can be found in the literature and in common discourse, demonstrating significant differences. The review cannot expect to be thorough, but operates using a selection of such elements, which will highlight the connections between the three concept-domains and their mutual interdependence, hopefully in a fruitful manner.

2.2.1 Innovation

A variety of definitions for innovation have been introduced, debated and criticized in both academic literature and popular press (e.g., in design research by authors such as: Hobday et al. 2011; Wylant 2008; Malins 2011; Storvang et al. 2014):

> Innovation is a process of turning opportunity into new ideas and of putting these into widely used practice (Tidd et al. 2005: 66).

> Innovation is the embodiment, combination, or synthesis of knowledge in original, relevant, valued new products, processes, or services (Luecke and Katz 2003: 2).

> All innovation begins with creative ideas. We define innovation as the successful implementation of creative ideas within an organisation. In this view, creativity by individuals and teams is a starting point for innovation; the first is a necessary but not sufficient condition for the second (Amabile et al. 1996: 1155).

> An important distinction, attributed to the innovation theorist Joseph Schumpeter, is normally made between invention and innovation. Invention is the first occurrence of an idea for a new product or process, while innovation is the first attempt to carry it out in practice (Fagerberg et al. 2013: 6).

Several categories of innovations have been identified and labelled with different purposes: e.g. Design-driven innovation, Innovation of meanings, Innovation of technology, Business Model Innovation, Economic Innovation, Scientific Innovation, Social Innovation, Technological Innovation, Data and Value Innovation etc. Each type of innovation has its own definition—e.g. Data innovation is defined as "data creates value of data for social and economic benefit" (Soto, Urbact II capitalisation 2013), the Value innovation is defined as "a change in parameters customers use to give value to products" (Verganti 2016a, b) and Social innovations are described as "innovations are social in both their ends and their means. Specifically, […] social innovations [are] new ideas (products, services and models) that simultaneously meet social needs (more effectively than alternatives) and create new social relationships or collaborations. They are innovations that are not only good for society but also enhance society's capacity to act." (European Commission Bureau of European Policy Advisors, BEPA, 2011, p. 9)

Innovation is therefore not limited to creativity or novel ideas or inventions, but also to market and value creation for individuals as well as for enterprises:

> Innovation is the successful creation and delivery of a new or improved product or service in the market …innovation is the process that turns an idea into value for the customer and results in sustainable profit for the enterprise (Carlson and Wilmot 2006: 3–4).

> Innovation is the multi-stage process whereby organisations transform ideas into new/improved products, service or processes, in order to advance, compete and differentiate themselves successfully in their marketplace (Baregheh et al. 2009: 1334).

All these definitions contain terms such as practice, implementation, valued products, processes or services that clearly indicate an orientation towards supporting practical outcomes that have a tangible impact. The approach we decided to adopt is precisely oriented toward igniting and sustaining innovation processes and projects that can have an impact in terms of proposing and creating value in a context of transitioning global values.

In his most influential writings, Verganti (2009), Verganti and Dell'Era (2014) presents innovation strategies, mostly focusing on what he calls design-driven innovation. He discusses two types of innovation in a design-driven context: (a) technology/solution innovation and (b) meaning innovation. Verganti's work emphasizes that innovation through solution and technological development lies in solving the established need, problem, or challenge in an incremental or radical way. However, when innovation springs from a novel vision of the user problem/need it can generate value by leveraging on individual and social meanings (values). Verganti describes meaning as follows:

> Meaning reflects the psychological and cultural dimensions of being human. The way we give meaning to things depends strongly on our values, beliefs, norms and traditions (Verganti and Dell'Era 2014: 52).

This means that technologies and solutions may be changing incrementally or radically, but the problem and meaning keep changing as well. Verganti elaborated further on this point of value innovation:

> Value innovation is a change in parameters customers use to give value to products (Verganti 2016a, b: 23).

A core idea of Verganti's reasoning is the assumption that design can play a crucial role in the process of generating and exploiting the innovation area related to meanings. His thesis is that design by creatively working on the social and emotional product attribution of value can be strategically used by firms in order to expand their market or even create new market areas by influencing new individual and societal needs. In this conceptualization great emphasis is given to creativity and "genius" as the key skills of the designer enabling her/his capacity to envision new possibilities:

> We understand creativity as the capacity to create, which is to produce a new knowledge or new meaning. This newness must be considered against the stock of scientific and cultural products existing in a given society. Innovation is the process by which, on the basis of creativity, new value is added to a product (good or service) or to the process of its production/distribution. Value can be exchange value (e.g. money) or use value (something useful for society, for some institutions, for some organization, for the individual, or for a collective of individuals) (Castells et al. 2017: 16).

Creativity has been and is largely considered relevant for innovation. Although creativity goes hand in hand with innovation, it is not innovation. While creativity is the ability to produce new and unique ideas, innovation is the implementation of that creativity—that is the introduction of that "new" (idea, solution, process, product, service…) into the real world (Gutzmer 2016).

Creativity is the driving force behind innovation and this is why some authors are considering creative jobs (Dvir and Shamir 2003) and creative classes (Florida 2002) relevant to the innovation ability of more or less complex organization. Usually this creativity is associated with specific people, individuals, operators, professionals, still some authors consider creativity as a relevant capacity of plural and multiple environments where creativity is considered a sort of phenomenon of the multitude, embedded in its diversity and interactive behaviours.

Open innovation represents the main output of an important transformation for innovation processes and activities; according to Gutzmer, it "essentially means opening up the laboratories of a company to forces from the real world—to other companies, to users […], to universities. All this is called "outside-in innovation" to be distinguished from "inside-out innovation" (p. 50), essentially the external exploitation of knowledge developed internally. The idea of open innovation demolishes any boundary between inside and outside in terms of value creation and moves it into the complexity of the open network where innovation takes place. Openness is a condition that can produce innovation but is not a guarantee for it to occur. Open innovation means that the link to the outside world has the capacity to allow for the imagination and creation of new values.

Although creativity and the attitude to merge and combine different areas of meaning and practice (bricolage, Grin et al. 2010) can definitively be considered central in the innovation process, it must be remembered that innovation is a non-linear process where causality is multidimensional and not easy to be established:

> Actors move back and forth between domains such as science, market, regulation and production. This undermined the idea of a neat and linear sequence of stages. Instead, technology and context were co-constructed in a messy process. Socio-technical innovation appeared to be a more systemic process of creating linkages and building heterogeneous networks. (…) Creativity and bricolage are important in these processes (Grin et al. 2010: 31).

The perspective introduced by Geels (2002) and Grin et al. (2010) provides an interesting framework to interpret innovation processes. The authors consider innovation as a multi-phase transition process. They hence identify four alternating phases:

(i) The pre-development phase from dynamic state of equilibrium in which the status quo of the system changes in the background, but these changes are not visible;
(ii) The take-off phase, the actual point of ignition after which the process of structural change picks up momentum;
(iii) The acceleration phase in which structural changes become visible;
(iv) The stabilisation phase where a new dynamic state of equilibrium is achieved (Grin et al. 2010: 4–5).

They consider innovation not only as a multi-phase, but also as a multi-level process: namely as *interference of processes at three levels: innovative practices (niche experiments), structure (the regime), and long-term, exogenous trends (the landscape)* (Schot 1998; Rip et al. 1998; Geels 2005, as in Grin et al. 2010: 4–5).

The three levels present different features (size, stability, practices, networks…) and contribute differently to the innovation process.

Niches are characterized by small and precarious networks. They hold onto widespread rules; activities are not structured or characterized by a high level of uncertainty (Grin et al. 2010). Nevertheless, niches are the incubators of innovation; they build up on local networks but can connect to global ones and provide the right conditions in terms of freedom and space for creative ideas to grow into innovations.

Socio-technical regimes present a more stable condition. They involve long-range networks and three types of stable rules (ibid.): cognitive (belief systems, guiding principles, goals, innovation agendas, problem definitions and search heuristics), regulative (regulations, standards and laws) and normative (role relationships, values and behavioural norms) (ibid 2010: 20–21 and Geels 2004 in Grin et al. 2010).

> The rules of socio-technical regimes account for the stability and lock-in of socio-technical systems.
>
> (…)
>
> As a result of these lock-in mechanisms, existing socio-technical systems are dynamically stable: innovation still occurs but it is of an incremental nature, leading to cumulative technical trajectories. Such predictable trajectories occur not just for technology, but also for policy, science, industry, culture and markets.
>
> (…)
>
> At times, however, changes in trajectories are so powerful that they result in mal-adjustments, tensions, and lack of synchronicities. These tensions create windows of opportunity for transitions (Grin et al. 2010: 20–21).

Conflict is a key element of transition; it is always present even when there is agreement on rules and practices. It becomes a key trigger of the transition process when actors start questioning basic rules and behavioural norms leading to structural regime crises (ibid. 2010).

Socio-technical landscapes are the most stable level and are identified as follows:

(1) factors that do not change or that change only slowly, such as climate;
(2) long-term changes (…);
(3) rapid external shocks, such as wars or fluctuations in the price of oil.

> This varied set of factors can be combined in a single "landscape" category, because they form an external context that actors cannot influence in the short run. This does not mean that landscape developments occur without human agency. Urbanization, globalization, environmental problems and macro-cultural changes obviously come about through aggregations of multitudes of actions (Driel and Schot 2005 in Grin et al. 2010: 24).

External landscape changes are the key factor creating pressure on existing regimes and unlocking them (Grin et al. 2010). This opens up different possibilities for niche-innovations to break through. Particularly Geels (2004 and in Grin et al. 2010) defines four transition pathways (Fig. 2.1):

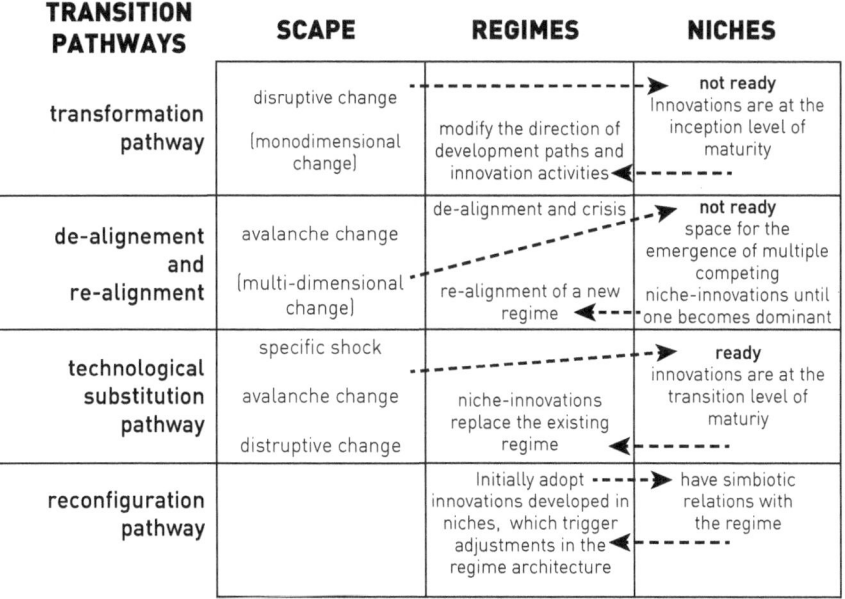

Fig. 2.1 Transition pathways (adapted from Geels 2005)

- Transformation
- De-alignement and re-alignment
- Technological substitution
- Reconfiguration.

Landscape pressure changes the actors' perceptions, negotiations and agenda setting and lead to particular windows of opportunity enabling innovation to scale-up:

- Users may change their preferences: (…) This leads to regime tensions when established technologies have difficulties to meet the new market demands.
- Continued expansion of regimes may lead to increasing negative externalities. (…)
- If regimes cause problems that are perceived to threaten society, policymakers may introduce new regulations that introduce performance standards that cannot be met by the existing technology.
- Continuing problems can undermine the trust in existing technologies and alter expectations in new technologies.
- Strategic games in industrial populations may also open up the regime (Grin et al. 2010: 25).

Landscape changes trigger the transition process, but it is the destabilization of existing regimes that constitutes the key to transitions (ibid. 2010: 79). When change alters the regime or a process of substitution is ignited, it means the amplitude of the transition is systemic and affecting several dimensions.

The three levels align through processes that have *evolutionary* characteristics:

Niches provide the locus for the generation of radical novelties (variation), but the selection and broader diffusion of these novelties depends on alignments with regime and landscape levels (ibid. 2010: 18).

Norgaard (1994) and more recently Harvey (2011) propose a co-evolutionary mode of change whereby different spheres of activity interact and change one another in a mutually constitutive manner. (…) Evolution means that epoch change, scape change, become evident with the passing of time; they are not perceptible as they happen. Within cultural dominant conditions, these spheres are interlocked and hard to change, giving the impression of an immutable system. (…) This hides the variation and the diversity that always exists or is being activated in each sphere. Such diversity is constantly renewed through pure novelty (mutation in biology), intentional or unintentional. Those variants of one sphere that best fit (as for complementarity, possible synergy, similarities, alignment….) the dominant ones of another are the ones more likely to survive and expand. Minoritarian interlocked sub-systems often co-exist "within the shell of the old" (…) developing in niches and expanding/outbursting when the surrounding conditions change (at landscape or regime level). Spatial separation facilitates niche differentiation and evolution. As new life forms have evolved in distant islands, new social and cultural forms may emerge in distant geographies or by groups that manage to spatially isolate and autonomise their territory, while networking to transfer its innovation (Castells 2017: 42).

Changes in administrative and institutional arrangements (regime change) cannot emerge alone and in the vacuum, without mutually constitutive changes in other spheres. The emergence of new alternative economic practices is the proof of new variants in some relevant spheres (Castells 2017: 50).

The latter may include labour, cultural systems, which are seeds for larger scale changes. There is evidences which supports a synergic combination and (even) an initial scaling up of such practices can activate important positive impacts on global challenges: Hlebik (in Castells 2017) shows for example the relevant impacts on macroeconomic features, on entrepreneurships, and even on climate and the environment of the adoption of complementary currency systems.

The conceptual framework defined by the aforementioned references enables us to position our reasoning on a sound basis. Aiming this book at an operational and praxis oriented approach, the proposed review is to be considered as a starting point for defining the key attributes of the innovation processes we aim at supporting.

It is therefore necessary to answer the question: What kind of innovation are we aiming at?

We chose to focus our definition selecting a few key concepts.

First, a starting point is to look at how far innovations are, to use Heidegger's term, 'de-worlded' from everyday life. Feenberg (1991, 1995) offers a powerful conceptual and analytical framework to assess the extent to which innovations are coupled or de-coupled from the continuum of everyday life. The essence of the framework is Feenberg's definition of 'technique'—which can be defined as the interplay between two forces: primary and secondary instrumentalisation. Primary instrumentalisation characterises technical relations in every society. It can be summarised in terms of four 'reifying moments' of practice:

- De-contextualisation—the 'de-worlding' of innovations. The extent to which innovations are separated from their context (e.g. the gentrification and 'disneyfication' of an old industrial district).
- Reductionism—the process in which the de-worlded things are simplified, stripped of 'technically useless qualities', and reduced to those aspects through which they can be enrolled in a technical network (e.g. automating a tram system).
- Autonomisation—dissipating or deferring feedback from the object of action to the actor (e.g. getting rid of or tokenising tenants consultation committees in housing regeneration).
- Positioning—the ways in which innovations turn the properties of an object to the laws and agendas of 'technicisation'—(e.g. using social media to create a network of surveillance systems in a city).

Secondary instrumentalisation can be seen as the oppositional dynamic to primary instrumentation. It also operates in a dialogue with primary instrumentalisation in four 'moments':

- Systematisation—the process of making combinations and connections between innovations and the natural environment. This leaves room for social interests and values to intervene in the innovation process.
- Mediation—ethical and aesthetic mediations supply the 'simplified technical object' (innovation) with new secondary qualities that reinsert it into its new social context.
- Vocation—'autonomisation' of the innovation is mediated through the acquisition of 'craft'. Acquiring vocational identity and skills engages people in a community which can then involve people in the lifecycle of innovations.
- Initiative—corresponds to 'positioning' but focuses on voluntary cooperation in the coordination of innovation effort. It has the potential for reducing alienation through substituting self-organisation for control from above.

In our view, the two dynamics need to act with synergy. While today's dominant idea of innovation tends to favour dynamics belonging to the primary instrumentalisation framework, since our reasoning is focused on tackling key societal and environmental problems, we find it crucial to shift the focus to features pertaining to the secondary instrumentalisation conceptual framework.

Second, although scholarly literature provides a wide variety of conceptualizations for the phases of innovation processes (e.g., technology push, market pull, linear model, simultaneous coupling, interactive model, architectural model, network model, open innovation S-shaped logistic function model, and many others; for a review of some of the models and some historical notes see: Tidd et al. (2005), Meissner and Kotsemir (2016), Godin (2017), we decided to adopt the idea of innovation as an heterogeneous multidimensional process as described by the multilevel concept by Grin et al. (2010) and look at innovation in terms of its stages of maturity in relation to different processes of transition.

Here we identify three stages of maturity:

- *Inception*: Experimental research; marginal practices; identification of market/societal needs; embryonic ideas;
- *Development*: from an idea to a product, service, project solution, consolidated practice, etc. Structured process of added value creation;
- *Transition*: scaling up, diffusion of the innovation in the native context and beyond; augmented adaptiveness of the solution and/or capability to substitute pre-existing socio-technical regimes.

Systemic change (scape change) is a fourth possible stage. It evolves from the intensive adoption of one or (more likely) several innovations, which can provoke simultaneous changes in the system (behavioural, cognitive, institutional, etc.) resulting, in the long-term, in a new scape configuration. This process cannot be designed as an act of intention, but just observed in its development. Nevertheless, it can be fuelled by several niche-innovations (Grin et al. 2010) aiming at changing practices and behaviours in the direction of the desired -scape change.

The maturity stages fit Geels' multi-level innovation model. As it is possible to map them in the three different levels (see Fig. 2.2) and identify the areas of transition between levels. We agree with Geels' assumption that the interface with regimes (in crisis or well-established) is the key factor for scaling up innovation, therefore niche-innovations, in order to dialogue with the regime, need to be at the stage of development: They need to be ready to be adopted through a conceivable process of translation into the regime rules or to constitute a new regime (Fig. 2.3).

Third, in this perspective there is no use in opposing radical and incremental innovation. In the document "Defining innovation in the context of the UIA Initiative, March 2017", two types of innovations are presented:

- Revolutionary innovations, which can be achieved by experimenting with new technologies or products or designing services to tackle new challenges or finding new ways to face old but unsolved ones
- Evolutionary innovations, which build up on past experiences trying to go beyond everything that has already been tested before.

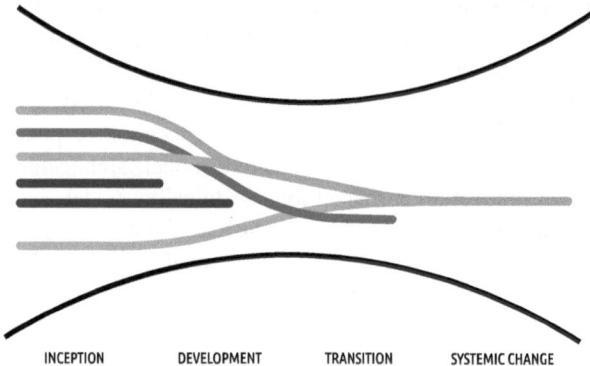

Fig. 2.2 Innovation maturity stages

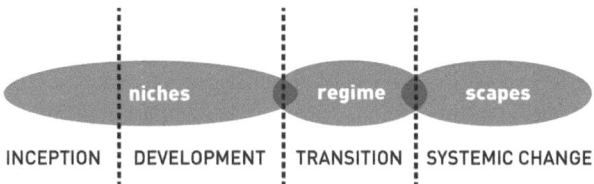

Fig. 2.3 Innovation maturity stages mapped onto Geels' multi-level model (adapted from Geels 2005)

Different types of innovation processes need to act at the same time in order to allow for a successful change to occur (Cruickshank 2014a, b). Radical innovation is often received positively, but that does not necessarily mean either economic or social success:

> Novelties may remain in niches for a long time. One possible reason is that technological development and trouble-shooting may last long (often decades). Another possible reason is that radical novelties face a mismatch with the existing regime, e.g. infrastructure requirements, user practices or policies that do not yet exist. At third possible reason is that existing regime actors actively oppose niche-innovations. Regimes may thus pose barriers for diffusion of niche-innovations. As long as existing regimes are stable, novelties have little chance to break through (Grin et al. 2010: 25).

> The term "radical" refers to the scope of change, not to its speed. Radical innovations may be sudden and lead to creative destruction, but they can also be slow or proceed in a step-wise fashion (Grin et al. 2010: 11).

This is relevant when designing innovation policies, which do not have to focus only on disruptive solutions, but also create the conditions for the creation of a favourable environment for a multitude of niche-innovations to emerge and grow into their various stages.

2.2.2 Design

> Design is a creative, analytical and problem-solving activity through which objectives and constraints are weighed and balanced, the problem and possible solutions explored and optimal solutions derived. The process of design should also add value to the individual component parts, so that the resulting whole is greater than the sum of the parts (Carmona and Tiesdell 2007).

> Good designers recognise pattern, construct ideas, add emotional feeling, including essence of operation, sensible, coherent, affordances, good design is an act of communication between the designers and the users. The good design must explain itself (Norman 2013).

> A process through which we consciously create possibilities (Metcalf 2014: vii).

> Design as a third culture (along with science and humanities). (…) A necessary human capacity (Banath, Cross in Metcalf 2014: vii).

Today's complex challenges also change the world with regards to design. The concept of design is changing rapidly. The traditional focus on products has moved to service design and to the design of product-service systems, combining both tangible and intangible elements. The focus on designing things nowadays includes designing complex networks of interactions as well. The design discipline is gaining wider attention, moving out of the workplace and embracing complex challenges. For many years, there have been several attempts at defining design, distinguishing the object of design and design as an activity, thus the design process and its outcome, as well as the role and skills of the designer. Traditionally, design has been conceived as a drawing, blue print, plan, model, layout, schematic, diagram, aesthetic, prototype and/or specifications produced to show the appearance, details of an object, product or thing before it is created/made/developed:

> Design is a broadly-defined activity that focuses on people in the process of defining new products and services; as a sector in its own right of specialised, professional economic activity, by trained and qualified practitioners and as a tool for business and organisational growth at the highest strategic level. In addition to its economic benefits, design also encompasses sustainable and responsible behaviour contributing positively to an innovative society and improved quality of life.[1]

In recent years a lot of attention has been focused on design as a potential contributor to business and public policy performance and consequently policies and actions have been promoted at the micro and global level in order to sponsor the adoption of design methods and tools by firms and organizations. Therefore, it is interesting to take a look into this trend, to understand in which way the concept proposed by this book complements and expands the design field of action.

The notion of design economy is particularly interesting when it comes to understanding the way design is commonly interpreted as a factor impacting on economic performance and indicators. The concept has been popularised by a 2015 publication[2] of the UK Design Council in an attempt to determine the economic value of design for Great Britain's GVA (Gross Value Added), exports, workforce, and productivity (GVA per worker). Before revealing its findings, the report tackled the issue of defining which industries held the highest intensity of design activities, measured by the share of people employed who could be considered to be involved in design-related occupations. The Eurostat database of the Specialised Design sub-sector summarises the EU28 Design Industries economic performance as follows: a little less than 180,000 enterprises (mostly SMEs) in 2015, up from 143,000 in 2012; about €26.5 billion turnover in the same year (compared with €19.5 in 2012) and more than 286,000 employees in 2016, growing from 210,000 in 2012[3].

---

[1]European Design Leadership Board, 2012, Design for Growth & Prosperity. https://publications.europa.eu/en/publication-detail/-/publication/a207fc64-d4ef-4923-a8d1-4878d4d04520 (accessed: December 2017).

[2]See https://www.designcouncil.org.uk/sites/default/files/asset/document/Design_Economy_report_web_Final_-_140217_Yea_1.pdf (accessed November 2017).

[3]https://www.econdb.com/dataset/SBS_NA_1A_SE_R2/annual-detailed-enterprise-statistics-for-services-nace-rev-2-h-n-and-s95/ (accessed November 2017).

While there can be mild disagreements on whether this sub-sector reflects the "true" perimeter of Design Industries—considering that it excludes, for instance, Architectural and Engineering design as mentioned above—a bigger challenge is to identify the sub-sector(s) fulfilling the definition of Design Intensive Industries. Good candidates in that direction are not only some other Divisions belonging to Section M—such as the already mentioned Divisions 71 "Architectural, engineering and technical consultancy services" or 72 "Scientific research and development"—but also some manufacturing industries or other service sub-sectors where the take-up of design can be considered very relevant, if not essential for the business performance of involved enterprises.

In addition, the relative heterogeneity of national definitions of occupations across Member States does not favour the comparability of findings, as highlighted by a 2012 survey of the United Nations[4]. However, even after a standard classification has been adopted, deciding if a certain occupation can be considered as design related proves to be another challenging matter. To some extent, a suggestion may derive from the subset of industries one has in mind to track, which however introduces a clear element of circularity: for instance, if we brought "Scientific Research and Development" (Division 72) to the forefront, then it would be quite obvious that an occupation such as "Research Project Manager" should be taken into consideration.

To exemplify the possible outputs of this endeavour, the following—certainly non-exhaustive—set of design-related occupations can be retrieved from the ISCO-08 database.

The list looks non-exhaustive, at least for not including skilled work or artisan occupations, which would add dozens of relevant items and make it even less manageable than it is now.

Whatever the adopted standard, using job- or task-related aspects as metrics implies establishing a many-to-many correspondence between Design Intensive, or even Non-Intensive industrial sectors and the various Design-related occupations. We see this endeavour as an iterative process, leading to solutions that may be locally satisfactory, but remain hardly comparable to each other, particularly across countries—not to mention diachronically, due to the evolving nature of the respective populations over time.

A last, but by no means least important, approach to collecting data on the use of design by enterprises is the execution of periodic or occasional surveys. Among the former, the Community Innovation Survey (CIS[5]) stands out since 1992 as a prominent example of systematic collection of information across all the EU Member States, plus some EFTA and some EU candidate countries, now being carried out every 3rd year (the most recent results are available as CIS 2014). Among the latter, several studies have been produced at national (single country)

---

[4]https://unstats.un.org/unsd/cr/ctryreg/ctrylist2.asp?rg=7 (accessed November 2017).
[5]http://ec.europa.eu/eurostat/statistics-explained/index.php?title=Glossary:Community_innovation_survey_(CIS) (accessed November 2017).

level, including: National Agency for Enterprise and Housing, 2003; Designium, 2004; Danish Government, 2007; Northern and Western Regional Assembly, 2015; CM International & PDR, 2015; see also the detailed list reported in BEDA, 2006. However, the Innobarometer surveys for 2015[6] and 2016[7] carried out for the European Commission by TNS Political & Social Network are noteworthy for two reasons: first, they include evidence from all EU28 countries, plus Switzerland and the US; second, the presented results show a decent consistency across the two years.

A common trait to all surveys, irrespective of their nature, is the tight connection between design and innovation activities. This connection has gradually received more and more emphasis across time. For instance, in CIS, 2010 design became, for the first time, part of the questions on expenditure for goods or services innovation ("*Activities to design, improve or change the shape or appearance of new or significantly improved goods or services*"), while 'aesthetic design' was still kept as example of marketing innovation. In CIS 2012 the question was modified again ("*Activities to design or alter the shape or appearance of goods or services*") but still included in the area of innovation as question #5.1, while question #9.1 on aesthetic design was still identical to that of CIS, 2008. In CIS, 2014 the question #5.1 still covered the design of goods and services, but the co-presence of the parallel question #9.1 as part of marketing innovation was acknowledged within the Methodological Notes as a likely source of uncertainty for the respondents:

> However, it may be difficult for respondents to distinguish between the concept of design in question 5.1 and aesthetic or stylistic changes for marketing purposes only. In general, updating an object or a space is a simple aesthetic change, for instance redecorating a hotel or changing the shape of the fenders on an automobile so that the automobile has a new style. Design, as covered in question 5.1, is more extensive, and involves either designing the appearance or shape of an object or service that is new to the enterprise, or changes to the shape or appearance of an existing object in a way that also improves ergonomic, ease of use or readability, or mass production characteristics. Many changes to packaging are only aesthetic. However, changes to the design of packaging to improve ergonomic, ease of use, or mass production characteristics fit under the concept of design covered in question 5.1 (CIS 2014a, b Methodological Notes: 7–8).

Against this background, worth noting is the emergence of a powerful scheme, which has become known as the Design Ladder. This was popularized in 2001 by the Danish Design Centre as an intuitive way of illustrating the growing engagement of enterprises in the use of design within their internal processes[8]. Basically, it is a maturity model, consisting of four steps, which are represented in the following picture.

---

[6]http://ec.europa.eu/COMMFrontOffice/PublicOpinion/index.cfm/ResultDoc/download/DocumentKy/67409 (accessed December 2017).

[7]http://ec.europa.eu/commfrontoffice/publicopinion/index.cfm/ResultDoc/download/DocumentKy/73869 (accessed December 2017).

[8]See https://danskdesigncenter.dk/en/design-ladder-four-steps-design-use (accessed December 2017).

Fig. 2.4 The Design Ladder (from an idea of the Danish Design Centre)

1. **No-Design**. Design is invisible, if used at all. Product or service innovation are not handled by professional experts. The user perspective plays little or no role;
2. **Design as Styling**. Design is seen exclusively as the final form-giving stage, be it in relation to product/service development or graphic design. Trained experts may or not be part of it;
3. **Design as Process**. Design is integrated since the early stages of product/service innovation. The solution is problem driven and/or user driven. Multiple skills and technical capacities are demanded and involved;
4. **Design as Strategy**. Design is adopted to rethink the business concept, vision, positioning in the value chain etc.—completely or in part (Fig. 2.4).

This scheme has contributed to complementing—and according to many, challenging—the CIS definition of design, in at least three respects:

- It has decidedly broadened the scope of design, from visual communication and aesthetic changes to existing products and services to the "creative problem solving" activity already mentioned in the first chapter of this Book;
- It has reinforced the connection between the use of design and the process of goods/ services innovation, as distinct from marketing, process and organizational innovation;
- It has explicitly introduced the user driven perspective into the more "mature" levels (3 and 4) of design use.

Interestingly enough, the Innobarometer surveys (2015, 2016[9]) have adopted the Design Ladder as a guideline for some of the design- and innovation-related questions. The definition of design used has been: "A range of applications within companies, providing a means to integrate functionality, appearance and user experience, for goods or services. Design can also provide a means to build corporate identity and brand recognition" (Innobarometer 2016: 94). The results are displayed for EU28 in the following adaptation of the previous figure.

---

[9]http://ec.europa.eu/growth/industry/innovation/facts-figures/innobarometer_en.

Of course, the distribution of responses across the Member States is far more heterogeneous than the above, but it is encouraging to note that the corresponding figures in the US benchmark (not shown in the picture) do not differ much from the EU28 average at each of the four steps (Fig. 2.5).

Another piece of evidence emerging from the surveys is the positive correlation (confirmed in both years) between a company's propensity to invest in design and the reported rate/frequency/speed of introduction of innovations in goods and/or services. While correlation is obviously not equivalent to causation, this is a strong argument in favour of the so-called non-R&D related innovation, which includes among other components (as implied by the CIS mentioned above) the implementation of design at a more mature level than the aesthetic one.

However, additional stylised facts can be inferred from the two surveys, notably that:

- Firms making a strategic use of design or which report using it regularly are much more likely to have introduced all types of innovation (including process, organizational and marketing design);
- However, companies that have introduced innovative goods or services are more likely than those who have introduced other innovations to say that design is a central element in the company strategy;
- The older the company, the more likely it is that design is not used;
- Smaller sized (micro) companies are more likely to say they do not use design than bigger (small to medium sized) enterprises;
- Firms from the industrial sector are more likely to report that design is not used internally than firms from other sectors;
- Companies with a falling turnover are more likely to say they do not use design than the firms with a growing turnover.

The data presented still reflects a view of design as an activity mainly (in some cases, exclusively) focused on products. Recently design became a holistic approach which allows for a range of considerations beyond aesthetics to be taken into account, including functionality, ergonomics, usability, accessibility, availability, product safety, sustainability, cost and intangibles such as brand and culture

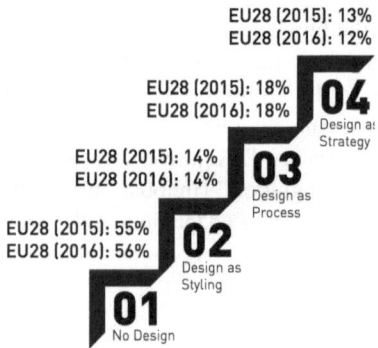

Fig. 2.5 Distribution of EU enterprises along the Design Ladder (*Source* Innobarometer)

[…]. A service designer may for example look at how a patient experiences the emergency service in a hospital or a visit to the bank. Similarly, urban designers look at how elderly or disabled people experience a visit to the town centre from an accessibility standpoint; business model designers are actively involved in organisational innovation; graphic designers work on visual communication of organisations, particularly in the creation and reinforcement of identities and brands, whether at the level of the organisation itself (cf. corporate identity) or at the level of its products, services or environments; an interface designer creates the visual language, the 'look and feel', of computer interfaces, whether for a website, software or a mobile device.[10]

Coherently design is increasingly recognised as a key discipline and activity for bringing ideas to the market, transforming them into user-friendly, appealing, high quality products or services. Although still often associated with aesthetics only, the application of design is much broader. It involves thinking from a number of disciplines, marketing and management among others, to strengthen the strategic perspective, as well as the social sciences and humanities, to understand the user. As such, design as a discipline is considered as the bridge between, for example, creativity and innovation, technology and the user, scientific and commercial disciplines. Design activities in general have user needs, aspirations and abilities as their starting point and focus and involve users in the process of co-design, co-creation and become important agents in innovation processes.[11]

Some relevant concepts, which demonstrate how much design is becoming pervasive and relevant at the same time, are shown in Table 2.1.

The previous definitions of, and references to, design from different documents and organisations within EC include some key aspects, that will be used to summarise a "working definition" of design and Design Enabled Innovation in this book (Table 2.2).

The most relevant features emerging from the above definitions are:

- *to be a human-centred activity,* which often implies the inclusion of users into the research and design phases of each innovation process.
- *to make use of specific operational tools* for researching, contextualising, modelling, testing and re-designing
- *to bridge the knowledge from different disciplines,* such as scientific, commercial and humanistic disciplines
- *to propose a holistic approach that links different aspects,* including functionality, ergonomics, usability, accessibility, product safety, sustainability, cost and intangibles, such as brand and culture.

---

[10]EC Staff Working Document, 2009, Design a driver of user-centered innovation. http://ec.europa.eu/DocsRoom/documents/2583/attachments/1/translations/en/renditions/native (accessed: December 2017).

[11]1st Action Plan of the European Design Innovation Initiative, 2011, https://ec.europa.eu/docsroom/documents/846/attachments/1/translations/en/renditions/native (accessed: December 2017)

Table 2.1 Detailed breakdown of design-related occupations

ISCO-08 code	English title
2141	Engineer, manufacturing
2142	Engineer, building structure
2143	Engineer, environmental
2144	Architect, marine/naval Designer, aircraft/engine/motor Engineer, aeronautical/aerospace/automotive/mechanical
2145	Technologist
2146	Engineer, mining/extractive
2149	Designer, non-computing systems Engineer, biomedical/nuclear/robotics
2151	Designer, engine/motor Engineer, electrical
2152	Engineer, electronics
2153	Engineer, telecommunications
2161	Architect, building/interior
2161	Architect, landscape
2163	Designer, industrial/product Designer, fashion/furniture/jewellery Designer, costume/dress/clothing/garment/textile
2164	Planner, land/town/traffic/urban
2165	Cartographer, Geodesist, Map Maker, Surveyor
2166	Artist, commercial/digital Author Designer, animation/computer games/graphic/multimedia/website Designer, poster/publication Illustrator
2511	Architect, business solutions/analysis Designer, IT/computer systems
2512	Designer, computer software
2513	Architect, information/computing/website
2521	Architect, database
3341	Planner, workforce
3432	Designer, interior/decoration/display/exhibition Designer, stage/set/scenery

Various design thinking and developing processes have been proposed, trying to operationalise the design creative process.

Brown (2009) proposes the three-step process, which covers inspiration, ideation, and implementation. Inspiration is defined as "the problem or opportunity that motivates the search for solution"; ideation is defined as "the process of generating, developing, and testing ideas" and implementation is defined as "the path that leads from perfect room to the market" An example of Nintendo Wii was given for the

Table 2.2 Concepts contributing to define "design"

Design capabilities	The ability of a subject to do something (Sen 2009). The design capabilities needed to carry out design activities. Competencies are recognized in three macro areas: Design Leadership, Design Management, Design Execution. Each of these is divided into one or more specific skills to explain the focus of the area • **Design Leadership** (holistic view, how people give meaning to things) is encountered when design participates in the strategic choices of the firm/organization, so that a design-driven innovation strategy is the core activity carried out through a people-centred approach • **Design Management** (visualising/materialising, managing the process) is the ability of managing design resources, in terms of human resources, design process and creativity, economic resources • **Design Execution** (applying new technologies) involves the presence of human resources with technical skills, design technologies and infrastructures, investments in the NPD process[a]
Design thinking	In the past few years, design thinking has become a mainstream idea in innovation and management, as demonstrated by the many articles that appear in newspapers and magazines such as Forbes[b], Fortune[c], or Fast Company[d], by dedicated special issues of Harvard Business Review[e] and by documentaries[f]. Design thinking has been widely promoted by authors such as Brown (2009), Roberto Verganti and Roger Martin (Martin 2009) among others. Brown, CEO of the design consultancy, IDEO, defines design thinking as "a discipline that uses the designer's sensibility and methods to match people's needs with what is technologically feasible and what a viable business strategy can convert into customer value and market opportunity" (Brown 2008, 86). Some commentators expressed concern over the way in which design thinking is presented in such outlets (Badke-Schaub et al. 2010; Deserti and Rizzo 2014; Johansson-Sköldberg et al. 2013; Nussbaum 2011). Design thinking is often seen as a practical toolkit that can be easily applied to radically transform business models and organisations. To use Ulla Johansson-Sköldberg and colleagues' words, the popular press tends to look at design imagining it as "a panacea for the economy" (Johansson-Sköldberg et al. 2013, 121), as something that could be rapidly deployed, for example, using freely downloadable PDF toolkits like the ones provided by the design consultancy IDEO[g]
Participatory design	Participatory design was developed in Scandinavian countries in the 1960 and 1970s as a method for working with trade unions[h]. It presents a set of tools to the assessment, design, and development of technological systems and organisations which support the active involvement of potential or current users (e.g. employees, partners, customers, citizens, end users) in the decision-making processes. The approach applies to various disciplines e.g. software design, urban design, architecture, landscape architecture, product design, sustainability, graphic design, planning. It aims at creating environments responsive and appropriate to the stakeholders' needs and values (cultural, emotional, spiritual, etc.)
Co-design	Co-design is an approach rooted in participatory design techniques. It presents a fundamental change in the traditional designer-client relationship (Chisholm, s.d.[i]). It aims at allowing the creative contribution of all affected stakeholders in the formulation and solution of a problem

(continued)

Table 2.2 (continued)

	Designers usually undertake the role of facilitators creating the conditions for people to interact, be creative, share insights and test new ideas (Chisholm, s.d.[j]) Different tools and techniques are available to support co-design processes (Tassi 2009 [k]): personas, storyboards, user journeys etc. Potential solutions can be tested through prototyping and scenario generation techniques (Chisholm, s.d.[l])
Open design	Open design is the development of physical products, machines and systems through use of publicly shared design information. Cruickshank (2014a, b: 51) identifies four different types of open design initiatives: 1. Customization: giving consumers the ability to modify objects that are produced in a central facility and shipped to the consumer 2. Distributed design: having systems of design where creative contributions after the point of sale are essential to complete the product 3. Open structures: the design of platforms, tools or methods that help non-professional designers create their own products (and potentially services), independent of professional designers who help create the system 4. Open access: (…) based on the premises that all that is required for open design is to make the means of production accessible to a wide variety of people

[a]DeEP—Design in European Policies, 2013, Glossary—http://www.deepinitiative.eu/ (accessed: December 2017)
[b]http://www.forbes.com/sites/reuvencohen/2014/03/31/design-thinking-a-unified-framework-for-innovation/#5bea94c056fc (accessed: December 2017)
[c]http://fortune.com/2015/11/16/ibm-discovers-design-thinking/ (accessed: December 2017)
[d]http://www.fastcompany.com/919258/design-thinking-what (accessed: December 2017)
[e]https://hbr.org/archive-toc/BR1509 (accessed: December 2017)
[f]http://designthinkingmovie.com/ (accessed: December 2017)
[g]https://www.ideo.com/post/design-kit (accessed: December 2017)
[h]http://cpsr.org/issues/pd/ (accessed: December 2017)
[i]http://designforeurope.eu/what-co-design (accessed: December 2017)
[j]Ibid
[k]http://www.servicedesigntools.org/taxonomy/term/1 (accessed: December 2017)
[l]http://designforeurope.eu/what-co-design (accessed: December 2017)

constraint and evaluation purpose involving desirability, feasibility (functional and technical details) and viability (cost/benefit analysis).

Another process proposed by Stanford University, which is known as the "design thinking model" includes the steps Empathy, Define, Ideate, Prototype, and Testing. Empathy is to understand user/market need, Define is the expectation and desire or specifications from the end user, Ideation is the capability for generating, developing, brainstorming, communicating, actualising ideas, Prototype is building the blueprint or 1st realisation of the products, tools or services and Testing covers the Acceptance Test, regulatory aspects, feedback, validation, evaluation, usability, functionality, quality check etc. The other design processes which are commonly used by architects, engineers, scientists and other thinkers to solve a variety of problems and come up with solutions include products, tools or software which meets certain specifications or criteria; the steps may include: defining the problem, collecting the relevant information and specifications, brainstorming and analysing the ideas, developing the ideas, getting feedback and improving the design. Another famous design process is known as "double diamond" from the Design Council UK[12]; its steps include Discover, Define, Develop and Deliver, a further detailed description of which is below:

- Discover includes initiating an idea, developing the concept, conducting market research, identifying the problem, or user needs;
- Define covers preparing the brief based on market research, requirements from the users, trends, focus group discussion and in-depth interviews, capturing every essential aspect of the design problem and writing initial specifications;
- Develop includes detailed designing, developing methods, processes, scheduling, producing the list of materials, logistics, tools, and time-to-market, building the products, measuring and performance testing, including self-test.
- Deliver includes delivering to user/customer and getting feedback, Acceptance from the customer/user, delivering, evaluating, further feedback and learning.

The concept of Design Enabled Innovation will consider such definitions in order to qualify existing or potential innovation processes (see Chap. 5).

2.2.3 Cities

Cities, as sophisticated artefacts, constructs or systems, have demonstrated that they are a very successful social organisation formula with an increasing attractiveness even in the worst situations (despite the fact that they also bring about all the hurdles and threats of the future). The world is, therefore, increasingly an urban world to the point that social, environmental and urban problems tend to be mixed together. Even a seemingly global issue, such as sustainability, could find its logical realm of resolution in cities. Cities, urban areas, and conurbations—diffused urban regions or megalopolises—are the indisputable protagonists of the 21st century. This seems to justify a great deal of efforts to understand the urban phenomenon in all its complexity and to move towards transversal knowledge of the city with a multidisciplinary approach.

The city cannot be seen as a simple geographical scape. Cities are in eternal becoming, never entering a stable state of being due to the rich, intense, open and evolving networks they are producers of, immersed in, and nodes of. Understanding cities involves considering a set of complex economic, social and cultural dimensions embedded in a certain spatial unit. As a consequence, the city as a concept and a living inhabited entity can be understood at least from a multidimensional perspective.

---

[12]https://www.designcouncil.org.uk/news-opinion/design-process-what-double-diamond.

First, the city is a spatial concept. Many scholars state that cities are, geologically, the settlement of inhabitants at a certain scale, which can be delimited by a range of criteria such as population size and density, urban function and policy, or historical traditions (Dijkstra and Poelman 2012; Parr 2007). For example, the updated definition adopted by the European Commission (EC) indicates the city and its related geographical area based exclusively on a population size and density (Eurostat 2016); in China cities are defined as a municipality directly under the Central Government, or a city or town established as one of the administrative divisions of the state according to its City Planning Law; in the United Kingdom, however, there are no clear criteria for identifying cities and the city status is conferred by Royal Charter. Furthermore, the spatial scale of a city is usually dynamic. On the one hand, it shows that the definition of a city changes over time in order to tackle emerging problems generated by the demographic dynamism of a population in flux (Otlensmann 1996). A recent example can be seen in the attempt of the European Commission and the Organisation for Economic Cooperation and Development (OECD) to develop a shared new definition of city in 2011, so as to achieve the feasibility and credibility of a cross-country comparison of cities within the OECD countries (Dijkstra and Poelman 2012).On the other hand, most cities originate from small historical urban centres and, then, connected, absorbed and merged their surrounding villages with the arrival of the industrial revolution and the growth in population. It was only during the 19th and the first half of the 20th centuries that many European cities reached anything near their current size.[13] Since then, both European and World cities have witnessed a constant increase in both urban and metropolitan areas. According to the United Nation, the world's cities with 500,000 inhabitants or more grew at an average annual rate of 2.4% between 2000 and 2016. In Spain, urban areas grew on average by 17.5% between 2000 and 2010 while French metropolitan areas grew on average by 4% between 1999 and 2007 (Duranton and Puga 2004). The urban has conquered any other inhabited space (Amin and Thrift 2002).

Second, the city is an economic concept. Cities are well distinguished from firms and corporate organisations as for their open nature, for the chaotic dynamics of their transformations, for the their tremendously vaguer value proposition and for the more fluid networking of their operators. Nevertheless, cities and companies are in strict relation: companies contribute to the creative capital of the city (Florida 2000), at the same time cities change companies as they allow the latter access to the wide, rich and intense networks they are active in (Gutzmer 2016).

Cities are, historically and globally, seen as an economic phenomenon. In Chinese the city itself, literally [chéng shì], is a compound word of the town [chéng] and the market [shì]. Such thinking is also widely involved in the rich Western literature. The classic sociologist Max Weber (1921–1969), for instance, argued

---

[13]See http://ec.europa.eu/eurostat/statistics-explained/index.php/Urban_Europe_%E2%80%94_statistics_on_cities,_towns_and_suburbs_%E2%80%94_patterns_of_urban_and_city_developments (accessed: December 2017).

that "cities originate in the trade and commerce consolidated in the hands of an urban aristocracy" and therefore, a city can be defined as "a settlement the inhabitants of which live primarily of trade and commerce rather than agriculture" (Weber in Sennett 1969). In his discourse, a city is a "market settlement" where inhabitants are frequently engaged in production and consumption activities based on regular rather than an occasional exchange of goods. Similarly, another prestigious urban scholar Jane Jacobs (1969) also suggested that a city—any city from ancient to modern—grew first through the production and import of goods for its own needs and thereafter for export to other cities, thus placing emphasis on economic attributes of city. From a more holistic perspective, the economic attribute of city is embedded in three dimensions of consumption, employment and workforce (Parr 2007). As far as consumption is concerned, most consumption takes place in the city. Cities have enough purchase power, more than that in rural areas, to create and support a supply of goods and services, thus cities become a consumption place for both urban and non-urban households. Regarding employment, cities provide most job opportunities and are a dominant source of employment for urban residents as well as residents in surrounding areas. With regards to the workforce, cities are also a major labour supply area for employment within and beyond city boundaries. Today, the above three dimensions of the city have been strengthened more than ever before thanks to convenient commuting due to the development of public transportation infrastructures; as a consequence, contemporary cities are playing a more and more important role in the regional economic development.

Third, the city is a social concept. Cities represent a way of life different from the countryside's. As the leading figure in the Chicago School of Sociology Wirth (1938) stated that it was the impacts of population features and their consequences, rather than urban population itself, that determined a city's characteristics as different from rural areas and among urban areas. Specifically, increasing population leads to individual variability, the relative absence of intimate personal acquaintanceship, and the segmentation of human relations; high-density of population diversified activities and increased the complexity of the social structure; heterogeneous populations heightened social mobility and ramified and differentiated the social stratification. Nowadays the "urban" as a pervading dimension and a way of life has conquered most of human settlements: *The city is everywhere and in everything* (Amin and Thrift 2002: 1). The city as a dense and single entity is still definable and the key place for looking at societal and economical change, and due to technological and social development, with local differences, a sense of the city is present in most of human interactions. Cities are hence closely linked to people. Humans are the subject of all economic, social and cultural activities and human practices on the city shape corresponding economic, social and cultural relations which ultimately define the function, symbol and character of a city; in this sense, people are the master of the city. In other words, cities should not be understood as a materialised object; instead, they are people-centred spaces.

Fourth, cities are a cultural concept. A city is a mapping of the relations between space and culture and different cities or different districts within a city may have different cultural features because of their space attributes. The American social scientist Borer (2006) summarised such relations of space and culture in six domains under an urban culturalist perspective. The first, images and representations of the city. The objects, images and symbolic expression of the city help people to identify the city and provide a means for personal and collective identification through connecting a city with specific cultural symbols, e.g. the Eiffel Tower for Paris, black taxis for London, La Sagrada Familia for Barcelona, and so on. The second, urban community and civic culture. Civic culture originates from urban communities and is rooted in the necessary interdependency and interaction of neighbours in the community. The third, place-based myths, narratives, and collective memories. Collective memory as a product of myth and narratives available publicly is stored and transmitted in and through places (e.g. city) and shared and diffused by and among local people (e.g. citizens), and ultimately helps to shape the sense of place and cultural identity among their inhabitants. The fourth, sentiment and meaning of and for places. In a broad sense, cities, like people, have certain ascribed statuses or levels of prestige by localizing themselves in some regional, national or global positions, such as the competition for capital of innovation or culture, or the ranking for global liveability. The fifth, urban identities and lifestyles. Only cities can provide *diverse* identities and lifestyles and allow for new subcultures because of a variety of population and their relations. The last, interaction places and practices. Cities provide a large amount of "third places" to host the regular, voluntary, informed and individual interaction of citizens beyond their "home" and "work" places. In one word, cities are places rich with meaning and value for those who live, work, and play in and near them (Borer 2006).

All in all, a city is a complicated economic, social and cultural phenomenon based on a relatively large and dense space where humans settle down for work and life. Considering the objective that this book wants to achieve, we tend to use the word city in its broad sense and stress its innovative implication of city in spatial, economic, social and cultural dimensions. The heterogeneity of cities is, in fact, the main indicator of the extent to which they are able to foster new lifestyles, new ways of seeing and living, new modes of coming together. From this perspective, cities represent the best places for innovation, as they integrate diversity through interaction and networks.

References

Amabile TM, Conti R, Coon H, Lazenby J, Herron M (1996) Assessing the work environment for creativity. Acad Manag J 39(5):1154–1184
Amin A, Thrift N (2002) Cities: reimagining the urban. Polity Press, Cambridge
Badke-Schaub P, Roozenberg N, Cardoso C (2010) Design thinking: a paradigm on its way from dilution to meaninglessness? https://www.researchgate.net/publication/265403729_Design_thinking_A_paradigm_on_its_way_from_dilution_to_meaninglessness
Baregheh A, Rowley J, Sambrook S (2009) Towards a multidisciplinary definition of Innovation. Manag Decis 47(8):1323–1339

Borer MI (2006) The location of culture: the urban culturalist perspective. City Commun 5 (2):173–197. Blackwell Publishing Inc

Brown T (2008) Design thinking. Harvard Business Review, June 2008

Brown T (2009) Change by design: how design thinking transforms organisations and inspires innovation. Harper Business

Carmona M, Tiesdell S (2007) Urban design reader. Architectural Press, Oxford, UK

Carlson CR, Wilmot WW (2006) Innovation: the five disciplines for creating what customers want. Crown Business

Castells M (ed) (2017) Another economy is possible: culture and economy in a time of crisis. Polity Press, Cambridge

CIS (2014) Community innovation survey. CIS 2014 harmonised questionnaire v13. Online: https://circabc.europa.eu/sd/a/34c6f294-fa27-4bb1-acf8-89a4b8a152ad/CIS2014_HARMONISED%20SURVEY%20QUESTIONNAIRE_v13.docx. Accessed Dec 2017

CIS (2014) Community innovation survey. CIS 2014 methodological notes for the questionnaire. https://circabc.europa.eu/sd/a/249f9013-5a7a-4c0c-8b6c-99f76a765dfa/CIS_2014_Methodological_notes_for_the_Questionnaire.pdf. Accessed Dec 2017

Cruickshank L (2014a) New design processes for knowledge exchange tools for the new IDEAS project. In: Paper presented at the creative exchange conference, Lancaster, United Kingdom. Design council UK

Cruickshank L (2014b) Open design and innovation. Facilitating creativity in everyone. Gower Publishing Limited, UK

Deserti A, Rizzo F (2014) Design and organisational change in the public sector. Des Mana J 9 (1):85–97

Dijkstra L, Poelman H (2012) Cities in Europe. The new OECD-EC definition. Regional focus, RF 01/2012, regional and urban policy. Retrieved 28 Jan 2015, from http://ec.europa.eu/regional_policy/sources/docgener/focus/2012_01_city.pdf

Duranton G, Puga D (2004) Micro-foundations of urban agglomeration economies. In: Henderson JV, Thisse JF (eds) Handbook of regional and urban economics, 1st edn, vol 4 (48), pp 2063–2117. Elsevier

Dvir T, Shamir B (2003) Follower developmental characteristics as predicting transformational leadership: a longitudinal field study. Leadersh Q 14:327–344

Eurostat (2016) http://ec.europa.eu/eurostat/statistics-explained/index.php?title=Glossary:Community_innovation_survey_(CIS). Accessed Nov 2017

Fagerberg J, Martin BR, Sloth Andersen E (2013) Innovation studies: evolution and future challenges. Oxford University Press

Feenberg A (1991) Critical theory of technology. Oxford University Press, New York

Feenberg A (1995) Alternative modernity: the technical turn in philosophy and social theory. University of California Press, Los Angeles

Florida R (2002) The rise of the creative class. Basic Books, New York

Florida R (2000) Competing in the age of talent: environment, amenities, and the new economy. A report prepared for the R.K. Mellon Foundation, Heinz Endowments and Sustainable, Pittsburgh

Geels FW (2002) Technological transitions as evolutionary reconfiguration processes: a multi-level perspective and a case-study. Res Policy 31(8–9):1257–1274

Geels FW (2004) From sectoral systems of innovation to socio-technical systems: insights about dynamics and change from sociology and institutional theory. Res Policy 33(6–7):897–920

Geels FW (2005) Technological transitions and system innovations: a co-evolutionary and socio-technical analysis. Edward Elgar Publishing, Cheltenham, UK

Godin B (2017) Models of innovation: the history of an idea. The MIT Press

Grin J, Rotmans J, Schot J (2010) Transitions to sustainable development: new directions in the study of long term transformative change. Routledge, New York

Gutzmer A (2016) Urban innovation networks, understanding the city as a strategic resource. Springer International Publishing, Switzerland

Harvey D (2011) The enigma of capital and the crises of capitalism. Profile Books

Hobday M, Boddington A, Grantham A (2011) An innovation perspective on design: part 1. Des Issues 27(4):5–15
Innobarometer (2016) http://ec.europa.eu/growth/industry/innovation/facts-figures/innobarometer_en
Jacobs J (1969) The life of cities. Random House
Jacobs J (1969) The economy of cities. Vintage Books
Johansson-Sköldberg U, Woodilla J, Çetinkaya M (2013) Design thinking: past, present and possible futures. Creat Innov Manag 22(2):121–146
Luecke R, Katz R (2003) Managing creativity and innovation. Harvard Business School Press, Cambridge
Malins J (2011) Innovation by design: a programme to support SMEs. Swed Des Res J 2:25–31
Martin R (2009) Design of business: why design thinking is the next competitive advantage. Harvard Business School Press
Meissner D, Kotsemir M (2016) Conceptualizing the innovation process towards the 'active innovation paradigm'—trends and outlook. J Innov Entrep 5:14
Metcalf GS (2014) Social systems and design. Springer, Japan
Norgaard RB (1994) Development betrayed: the end of progress and a coevolutionary revisioning of the future. London and New York, Routledge.
Norman DA (2013) The design of everyday things. Basic Books, The MIT Press
Norman DA, Verganti R (2014) Incremental and radical innovation: design research vs. technology and meaning change. Des Issues 30 (1):78–96
Nussbaum MC (2011) Creating capabilities. The human development approach. The Belknap Press, Harvard University Press, Cambridge
Otlensmann JR (1996) The new central cities. Implications of the new definition of the metropolitan area. Urb Aff Rev 31(5):681–691
Parr JB (2007) Spatial definitions of the city: four perspectives. Urb Stud 44(2):381–392. https://doi.org/10.1080/00420980601075059
Rip A, Kemp RPM, Kemp R (1998) Technological change. In: Rayner S, Malone EL (eds) Human choice and climate change. Resources and technology, vol II, pp 327–399. Battelle Press, Columbus, Ohio
Scholl B (1995) Aktionsplanung: zur Behandlung komplexer Schwerpunktaufgaben in der Raumplanung, ETH Zurich
Schot J (1998) The usefulness of evolutionary models for explaining innovation. The case of the Netherlands in the nineteenth century. Hist Technol Int J 14 (3):173–200
Sen A (2009) The idea of justice. The Belknap Press, Harvard University Press, Cambridge
Sennett R (ed) (1969) Classic essays on the culture of cities. Prentice Hall, New York
Soto P (2013) Cities of tomorrow—action today. URBaCT II Capitalisation. Key messages. http://urbact.eu
Storvang P, Jensen P, Christensen PR (2014) Innovation through design: a framework for design capacity in a danish context. Des Manag J 9(1):9–22
Tidd J, Bessant JR, Pavitt K (2005) Managing innovation: integrating technological, market and organisational change, 3rd edn. Wiley, Hoboken
Tassi (2009) http://www.servicedesigntools.org/taxonomy/term/1
Verganti R (2009) Design-driven innovation: changing the rules of competition by radically innovating what things mean. Harvard Business School Publishing, Boston
Verganti R, Dell'Era C (2014) Design-driven innovation: meaning as a source of innovation. In: The Oxford handbook of innovation management. Oxford University Press
Verganti R (2016) Overcrowded: designing meaningful products in a world awash with ideas. The MIT Press
Verganti R (2016) The innovative power of criticism. Harv Bus Rev, January–February Issue
Wirth L (1938) Urbanism as a way of life. Am J Sociol 44(1):1–24
Wylant B (2008) Design thinking and the experience of innovation. Des Issues 24(2):3–14

Open Access This chapter is licensed under the terms of the Creative Commons Attribution 4.0 International License (http://creativecommons.org/licenses/by/4.0/), which permits use, sharing, adaptation, distribution and reproduction in any medium or format, as long as you give appropriate credit to the original author(s) and the source, provide a link to the Creative Commons license and indicate if changes were made.

The images or other third party material in this chapter are included in the chapter's Creative Commons license, unless indicated otherwise in a credit line to the material. If material is not included in the chapter's Creative Commons license and your intended use is not permitted by statutory regulation or exceeds the permitted use, you will need to obtain permission directly from the copyright holder.

Chapter 3
Cities as Enablers of Innovation

Grazia Concilio, Chuan Li, Pau Rausell and Ilaria Tosoni

3.1 Innovation and Cities Interplay

Cities embody an organisational climate (Jacobs 1969a) enabling and catalysing innovation and are by nature innovation generative systems They are considered key environments for the emergence of innovative interactions and relationships: creative and innovative industries tend to localize in or in proximity of urban environments, thus taking advantage of shared knowledge and a density of specialised and potential customers, suppliers, designers, experts and workers to create new tools, technologies, methods, instruments, products, processes, policies and services (Asheim et al. 2007; Pratt 2008; Reimer et al. 2008; Stam et al. 2008; Therrien 2005). Innovation processes in cities benefit from the diversity and accessibility to modern infrastructure, providing a range of stimuli (and recent research looks at such stimuli as positive externalities) which in larger cities are richer in number and potential: firms operating in big cities tend to be more innovative, agile and creative than in small ones (Duranton and Puga 2004; Stolarick and Florida 2006).

Furthermore, cities hold the "right" mix and concentration of resources to trigger, generate, foster and catalyse innovation, but also the greatest need to face the large challenges related to sustainability and economic and social justice (Dvir and Pasher 2004).

The vibrant relationship between innovation processes and urban dynamics is often questioned as a key factor in the attempt to promote positive change both in

---

G. Concilio (✉) · I. Tosoni
Politecnico Di Milano, Milan, Italy
e-mail: grazia.concilio@polimi.it

C. Li · P. Rausell
University of Valencia, Valencia, Spain

terms of economic development and sustainable solutions to societal and environmental problems.

> Cities provide an ideal environment for innovation as they offer proximity, density and variety (Athey et al. 2008).

Cities are therefore scanned thoroughly in order to sense all potential cues of their capability to set the innovation cycles in motions. They are mainly considered to be *cauldrons* (Leon 2008) where the combination of people, organisations, resources and infrastructures generates a *turbulent ecosystem (environment)* which in turn fuels creative processes (Johnson 2008). As Athey et al. (2008) point out, in this view, cities support innovation indirectly by acting both as *urban hubs* and *local links*. The capacity of cities to act as hubs resides in their role as gateways to accessing different *markets* (local, regional, national and international) combined with a series of urban *assets* (infrastructures, property, skilled workforce). On the other hand, they provide *links* to specialized *networks* (formal/informal, public/private) and *institutions* (government, agencies, ...), which can be critical in the different phases of the innovation process to enhance a creative idea from a seminal development stage to its consolidation and dissemination (e.g. by adding inputs and contributions from different areas of knowledge and expertise or by levering innovation up to provocative institutional change).

Furthermore, the correlation between cities and innovation in present times can also be regarded from a different perspective. In times of vital rethinking of our development patterns in order to contrast global warming and its several threats, cities are themselves concrete material for innovation:

> Cities are good at generating problems and the city fabric is problem-rich. Large groups of people living and working in close proximity put strains on natural resources and energy. Congestion puts transport systems under stress and the high costs of land mean intense land use. While individual consumption of land and the natural environment may be relatively low, total consumption in cities is very high. Air pollution, insufficient waste treatment and high contamination levels may engender health problems, for example. Furthermore, in cities, redistribution of income and power between persons and organisations with different innovation and learning capabilities lead to conflicts and undermines social capital. This is a general phenomenon in the globalising learning economy, but it is accentuated in cities (Johnson 2008).

Being the areas where problems related to unsustainable resource consumption (soil, energy, water, food, ...), congestion, air pollution, migrations, social exclusion ..., assume a critical dimension in terms of actual liveability, cities challenge the same concept of innovation by adding a feature of long-term positive effects to the innovation social assessment framework. Urban populations make sense of innovation in the framework of their complex mental map of physical and social relations. In order to be accepted an innovation has to potentially become functional to a "way of" living the city deeply rooted in the behavioural patterns of its inhabitants, or to be so far-reaching to induce a process of behavioural change. Cities therefore become the final testbed for innovation produced elsewhere or with no sense of urban dynamics and, at the same time, they nest/incubate sprouts of innovation generated from the city's capability of creative problem solving.

The city is hence a hotbed for creativity and innovative culture and a place where different operating groups (companies, public authorities, NGOs, citizens, start-uppers, entrepreneurs etc.) receive continuous stimuli to engage in product or service innovations that fulfil specific needs (market, organisational or community).

This creative process generates a constant need for *learning and relearning* the inhabited space by different people as a response to different needs (McFarlane 2011) and as a reaction to innovation generated within or imported into the city. Through this continuous activity of re-setting and re-defining (design) networks, tools and (political) agendas the city is described as a *learning machine* (McFarlane 2011): a tightly coupled combination of systems, which react and adjust to change, generated through the direct experience of being involved in the production of new knowledge and learning which is connected to the transformative process of innovative ideas into new products, services, procedures, organisations. The city itself is hence defined as a *territorial system of innovation* (Johnson 2008): a complex and dynamic framework *that includes people, relationships, values, processes, tools and technological, physical and financial infrastructure* (Dvir and Shamir 2003; Dvir and Pasher 2004). It is therefore the ability of the system as a whole to produce new knowledge and cope with change that defines its *innovation performance* (Johnson 2008).

As a consequence, whether innovation is generated by networks within the city (firms, groups of citizens, scholars, institutions) or imported from other networks or cities, a phase of embodiment in urban knowledge is crucial and constitutes a specific phase of product development, whose outcomes can be much different from the original idea. These non-linear and unpredictable developments are distinctive of urban dynamics, where a multitude of actors work together with their creative energy, implicit/tacit design capabilities, shared problem-solving strategies, propensity to learning and experimenting, capacity to generate new, economically sound and valuable solutions and ultimately growth and jobs for themselves and other people.

Cities are also places in which periods of relatively high and diffused welfare can suddenly be interrupted by outbursts of stagnation or crisis, putting pressure on the public sector's budgets, especially in delicate areas such as unemployment and social or environmental services. These phenomena are also generative of innovative ideas produced by local institutions, but mainly by active local communities, who can be facilitated or prevented in their operations by context-specific conditions.

The type of knowledge produced through these processes is, as a result, *spatially sticky* (Johnson 2008): its key features are rooted *in the minds and bodies of agents, in the routines of firms and, not least of all, in the relationships between people and organisations*. This makes the transfer and portability of ideas and solutions, from one city to another or to a different context, a complex process, which might involve a significant rethinking of the original concept.

Analysing the elements of the interplay between the city and innovation processes is the gateway for Design Enabled Innovation initiatives to be scaled up or replicated across different contexts.

3.2 Five Interfaces of the City Relevant for Innovation

In the search for the most significant elements/components/areas of interaction between the city and the development processes of new ideas, products, services, etc. distinctive urban elements can be considered as relevant. To these components pertain specific resources which separately, but more often in combination, can fuel the idea and product development process increasing the generated added value. It is in these areas that *'hidden, scattered and badly utilized resources'* (Hirschman 1958*)* can be identified and mobilized in order to boost the creative process. A process that, according to the specific situation of the urban context can be initiated both by supply (firms, public or private institutions) and demand (groups of citizens, associations, consumers,…) (Johnson 2008).

Every city presents a specific combination of these layers of attributes, which ultimately describe its unique identity and its potential capability of enabling the conditions for creative innovation processes to set-in.

Five of these dimensions could be especially significant in relation to Design Enabled Innovation: 1. The City as a market place; 2. The City as a problems lab; 3. The City as an idearium; 4. The City as a resource pot; 5. The City as a political arena.

Historically cities are market places, areas where people gather to trade and make deals. Access to differentiated markets is one of the greatest advantages of urban locations (Athey et al. 2008). Firms can benefit from the proximity to a significant choice in terms of suppliers, labour and costumers and thrive from the interaction with demands and offers coming from local and global markets which have their terminals in the city.

A particular type of market, subject to its own rules, is the labour market. Cities differ in work culture and can develop specific environments characterised by the concentration of specialised competences and skills connected to a certain industrial/service sector or to a recurring organisational pattern. These environments can promote and support (or hinder) the exploitation of creative ideas leading to production and to organisational and spatial change.

When talking about innovation, financial markets and, particularly, access to financial resources and funding is crucial:

> Stock exchanges, banks, joint venture funds and other financial institutions can serve as engines for innovation. However, the potential of these institutions to drive innovation should not be taken for granted - it requires smart, responsible and innovative attitude from all the stake-holders (Dvir and Pasher 2004).

Markets not only work as suppliers of resources and selling opportunities for companies, they also act as demand generators. Stimuli to develop new products, ideas and creative networks can originate from market trends (both successes and failures) and analysis. This is nevertheless a simplified way for companies to look at the urban sphere: As a static and easy to handle system for marketing. This can mislead choices and decisions for innovation to be scaled up in urban environments. The urban sphere and its complex networked nature interact with human knowledge to determine behavioural patterns which are hardly interpreted by statistical analysis, but rather related to the way individuals relate to the networks and interact through them.

On the other hand, hints can also come from marginal and hidden niche-markets. The urban market is particularly dynamic in this sense. Cities often present lab-like situations (informal markets, trading zones, Balducci 2001) where firms' contribution can be crucial to bringing an idea to life and at the same time represent a market to be developed for innovative companies.

Awareness on emerging new needs can create opportunities for new lead-markets to settle–in through the creation of innovation networks (Cappellin et al. 2015).

The city as a problem lab is naturally design-oriented. The wicked (or ill-defined) nature of urban problems (Ritter and Webber 1973) can only be fully understood by attempting their solutions. This means constantly revolving from the problem definition to the solution area, creating cycles of experiential learning (Kolb and Fry 1974; Stradtemeier et al. 2010).

Understanding problems by attempting solutions for them represents a way cities can develop experimental and learning abilities. This requires full awareness of the complexity and uncertainty of any city transformation and, at the same time, of the innovation potential of experimental approaches to problem solving. Awareness of global problems as drivers of change, such as climate change and peak oil consumption, demographic change, social inclusion and equity, globalisation etc. needs to be translated into the local framework of opportunities and resources available, as well as into the situated problem definition (Pinnegar et al. 2008). Innovation in these cases might mean to rethink the built environment, mobility modes, consumption patterns, urban behaviours, etc. Cities are places where new lifestyles and production systems are, and can be, tried out. They are the meeting points for those who share a common vision on problem and believe to be able to promote such significant changes. Thus what is interesting is that the precise way in which cities play out their laboratory function significantly depends of the way they are able to work on self-definition. Change quite often comes in the form of "what a city could be" according to an operational definition of its main problems/opportunities.

For instance, Schindler (2016) discussing the several options for reducing water and energy consumption in lawns keeping, investigates several experimental options for changing this practice of American identity. Here, experimental, laboratorial initiatives have both the role of better learning about the problem as well as developing a different identity practice. In a sense, in the laboratorial approach, the potential for achieving value creation is embedded in addressing global challenges and at the same time targeting practices.

Furthermore, the *city as an idearium* refers to both the diffuse ability of a city to envision solutions to the high number of problems it generates and the capacity of cities to catalyse creative energies, mainly by attracting skilled work-force.

In the knowledge economy the capability of a context to develop tradable concepts and design solutions by enabling competent actors is key to the success of a local *system of innovation* (Johnson 2008). Cities are the places where ideas and knowledge are produced, processed, exchanged and marketed (Van Winden 2014). The capacity of a city to favour the flourishing of creative thinking and to support the production of knowledge is a key anchor for innovation processes to nest in.

The idearium is the interface between local, situated networks and general thematic ones. The openness of the system towards inputs coming from the outside expands local innovation capacity. New information technologies permit the simultaneous dispersion and concentration of economic activity, which allows producers in large, productive urban centres to benefit from local knowledge flows by remaining anchored to a specific location, as well as to global knowledge flows and markets (Castells 2001). Cities, through their hub function, facilitate the access to knowledge networks and provide visibility to ideas in search of willing developers. Innovative firms can benefit from this environment by being able to integrate external sources of knowledge in their internal processes or to change them accordingly (Simmie 2003).

Cities differ significantly in their capacity to provide access to this kind of input. Knowledge networks in the city can be open and easily activated both by niches and regimes, but networks can also be closed and reluctant to interact with outside members. Furthermore, this field also presents a tendency towards resource concentration: "*The minority of cities at the top of the emerging 'international hierarchy of regions' tend to transfer specialized knowledge among themselves*" (Wolfe and Bramwell 2008: 176). The openness of high added-value knowledge networks is hence a critical indicator of a city's attitude towards innovation. Nevertheless, innovation processes can be set in motion also by non-expert knowledge and intuition. It is therefore interesting to look at niches, when thinking about ideas and knowledge generation, including from a social and spatial point of view. In fact, one of the reasons for the city's capacity to enable creativity is its richness in so-called "third places" (Dvir and Pasher 2004): spaces offering a comfortable time-space, where diversity and connection can inspire spontaneous creation processes and a feeling of safety can allow risk taking, informal knowledge management, interaction and contemplation. The city culture towards these kind of places is telling of an environment rich with opportunities for the sharing of ideas and their enactment.

The city as a resource pot considers the several resources available within a city framework both in terms of quality and variety. Besides knowledge and ideas, cities offer access to various assets that can be critical inputs of the innovation process. Among others, the most significant can be:

- People, with their creativity and talent;
- Financing: From Maecenases, to innovation policies in the cities;
- Research institutions: universities, innovative clusters, hubs for innovations; Universities and higher education institutes are key actors in urban knowledge networks. Athey et al. (2008) identify four key functions of research institutions in promoting innovation:
  - source and main driver of commercial innovation potential;
  - hub for networking, collaboration and knowledge exchange;
  - providers of collective goods (e.g. equipment- including prototyping technology, virtual conferencing facilities and virtual design studios to facilitate real-time collaborative working across large distances);
  - founders of innovation communities.
- Infrastructure: physical and social networks; public and private services and facilities;
- Place: estates, working spaces, laboratories, meeting places, conference halls, etc.
- Symbolic meanings: if creative processes can be understood as the recombination of previous elements with new meanings, it is evident that the spaces themselves constitute cultural repositories that can be reused in new cultural processes in innovative ways.
- Lifestyles. Urban lifestyles advocate freedom, openness, novelty and mobility. Therefore, people living and working in the urban environment are more prone to change and innovation.
- Knowledge as the key resource made available in the city: it is not to be considered available in terms of knowledge management tradition, rather referring to the constant re-creation of the urban sphere by means of knowledge flows, thus implying a different notion of knowledge more coherent with the "compositional knowledge" which Amin and Thrift (2002) consider, knowledge with its sources, associations, and relations, i.e. knowledge flows within the network.
- Power: openness and transparency of decision-making processes; openness of the institutional framework (regimes);

The listed resources are of different nature and all interconnected. They can be mobilised individually or in synergy with different levels of intensity: regimes usually have a greater power on resource mobilisation, while niches can exploit them creatively in order to support the value generation process. Coalitions of operators can be created in order to access or manage a specific resource. The way through which each city is able to activate its own resources is revealing of its attitude towards action and change.

Lastly, the problems of maintaining urban order are not necessarily solved by technical innovations alone. Often both problem and solution are more institutional than technical, while conflicts and disagreements about the distribution of costs, benefits and power often block the solutions and make administrative and political change essential (Johnson 2008).

Going back to the seminal work of Mintzberg (1985), which gives us a comprehensive study into organisations, a political arena is raised when politics and conflict capture an organisation as a whole or significant part. Mintzberg identifies four forms of political arena (p. 141): *confrontation*, which is characterized by conflict that is intense, confined, and brief; *shaky alliance*, which is characterized by conflict that is moderate, confined and possibly enduring; *politicized organisation*, which is characterized by conflict that is moderate, pervasive, and possibly enduring; *complete political arena*, which is characterized by conflict that is intense, pervasive and brief. All four forms are characterised by diverse conditions and geographies of conflict, and also shape coalitions in the organisation that activate political discourses varying from specific problematic situations to ideological and value-related issues. Moving to urban environments, the political arena is any space-time opportunity for public debate regarding the common good. Political arenas in cities have the power to shape the urban political agenda: their conflictual/debating nature can be the consequence or driver of innovation initiatives. Political arenas, in fact may have a top-down or a bottom-up origin depending on the change pathway activated in the socio-technical system: they will be activated by a regime in the case of a transition pathway, while in the other instances the arenas will be activated by niches. In all cases they swing between regime and niches, they represent the opportunity for innovation and change to achieve transformation at regime scale.[1]

Relevant to this interface is the ability to manage and deal with conflicts and disputes in a way which is productive of knowledge and reflective of values thus developing the largest possible advantage from it, i.e. transforming it into *InnoCracy* spaces (Dvir and Pasher 2004), i.e. spaces for a democratic approach to innovation and change in response to contemporary global challenges.

Finally, due to their debating, the political arena represents the spatial and temporal sphere for developing collective and shared knowledge on values, introducing the scape as the leading element of knowledge production dynamics.

In conclusion, the five dimensions can be defined as interfaces through which the city interacts with innovation processes. Those processes vary significantly

---

[1]An elucidating example of the creation of a political arena is given by Nelson and Ehrenfeucht (2016) and the re-settlement strategy in Louisiana to deal with the higher frequency of hurricanes, which highlight that people oppose relocation in principle and take reflective actions that respond to their specific situations and their knowledge about likely future conditions, including when to accept or oppose relocation. People's situations and perspectives change over time forcing them to make decisions in dynamic circumstances. Decisions in such conditions are generative of a political arena where reflections do not only touch individual spheres of action (families and their choice between relocation or staying) but they include the larger community levels as well as the institutional dimension (possible policies to sustain different options, to face new probable events, to re-think institutional roles and efforts, to guarantee equity and security to the entirely exposed territories).

depending on the maturity stage and the way the innovation process enters the city through its networks.

A common feature in almost all elements informing these interfaces is that of being terminals or hubs of local and global networks. Connected to the five interfaces is in fact the networked nature of cities (Castells 1996, 1997, 1998): networks are the way those interfaces work. Cities are spaces of flows (1996) enabled in their growing intensity by communication networks. Communication networks are not space-indifferent: rather they are made of situated hubs (the cities themselves!) where these networks interweave. In these situated hubs different relations and different hierarchies between them are activated (Amin and Thrift 2002) so that every new relation that connects to a city, becomes part of its network, i.e. part of the city and its intrinsic capacity (intrinsic to a network) to create and recreate knowledge.

The global city is a productive entity in which individuals (with different skills and abilities) create networks for the exchange of knowledge, financial resources, and products. It is in the city that the combination of different resources and dimensions generates different kinds of networks relevant to innovation processes; on one hand, business networks help co-ordinate decisions made by individual entities (people, firms or institutions); on the other hand, knowledge networks enable the transmission of data, information, and knowledge (Lambooy 2010; Martin and Simmie 2008). Urban proximity and connectivity help business and knowledge networks to form. Proximity also helps creating a shared sense of identity, which binds different players together in a community-like social network (Athey et al. 2008). One of the most relevant functionalities of cities is to provoke possibilities of interaction, cross-fertilisation and direct collaborations between different actors. It is precisely in this functionality that the connection between individual creativity and its social contextualisation lies. Aspects such as the density of stimuli, the creation of formal and informal meeting areas, the management of access flows or relations with the urban context act as conditions which potentially promote or limit the possibilities of materialization of a given level of relational capital.

These networks make the city a permanently changing, unstable set of forces and potentials seen as a never-ending project in the eyes of all involved (Gutzmer 2016).

The urban sphere is a cultural element that cannot be reduced to one set of key features. It is open to interaction with every other social or cultural sphere acting inside or outside it. Being complex open systems cities do not have a clear inside or outside which allows them to activate strong interconnections among many spheres as well as learning opportunities at several different levels of the network for all the spheres connected to them.

As innovation is clearly an issue of knowledge management for (new) knowledge creation, it is crucial and strategic to any organisation aiming at innovative production, to be effective in plugging into such networks, aware that they have no stable hierarchies and that they are constantly remodelled by means of networking improvisation (Gutzmer 2016), continuous linkages and de-linkages taking places within these hubs.

3.3 Scaling Innovation Up and Out Among Cities

Networks make the city a permanent changing, unstable set of forces and potentials seen as a never-ending project in the eyes of all involved (Gutzmer 2016) actors.

The urban sphere is a cultural element that cannot be reduced to one set of key features. It is open to the interaction with every other social or cultural sphere acting inside or outside it. Being complex open systems cities, do not have a clear inside or outside so being in the conditions to activate strong interconnections among many spheres as well as learning opportunities at several different levels of the network for all those spheres connected with them.

As innovation is clearly an issue of knowledge management for (new) knowledge creation, it is crucial and strategic to any organization aiming at innovative production, to be effective in plugging in such networks being aware that they have no stable hierarchies and that they are constantly remodeled by means of the networking improvisation (Gutzmer 2016), continuous linkages and de-linkages taking places in these hubs. These mechanisms and dynamics are crucial to scaling up and scaling out innovation as well as to urban economies.

In her seminal book on The Economy of Cities, Jacobs (1969b) presented an original narrative on why and how some cities grow and others stagnate and decay, based on a critical reading of earlier contributions by many scholars—historians and archaeologists in particular. Jacobs argues that the explosive economic growth derives from urban *import replacement* which occurs when a city begins to locally produce some goods that it formerly imported; this concept can be considered seminal for visualizing and interpreting contemporary dynamics of innovation scaling up and scaling out within urban economies.

In the mid-20th century Tokyo imported a lot of bicycles, which created a large market for repair shops. Eventually, those shops began making their own parts, which led to directly manufacturing whole bicycles and later exporting them. According to Jacobs, import substitution, however, can only happen in a large city or metropolitan area, for two main reasons: (1) small sized towns or rural villages are unlikely to generate enough demand for imported goods (e.g. bicycles and their spare parts), a necessary condition for import substitution to occur in the future; and (2) only large cities can provide the local culture and dense network of spatial relationships required to establish manufacturing where it did not exist before (e.g. teaching factory workers how to transform the components of a bike into a full product). As a matter of fact, Jacobs' distinction between cities (and metropolitan areas) on the one hand, towns and villages (small towns) on the other, is not based on the size of population or the territorial extension, but uniquely on the capacity that the former, not the latter settlements may have to generate stable growth and job opportunities from their own local economies.

Jacobs also claimed that not only does an increased local production of goods and services create extra value to the city (because, in our previous example, the price of an assembled bicycle in Tokyo is higher than the total cost of all its components, even if still imported), but this extra value is actually spent, at least in part, on different goods and services that are still produced in other cities, thus replacing old with new imports in a way that does not penalize cross-city trade, creates further opportunities for local industry to engage in urban import replacement, and ultimately produces a self-reinforcing cycle of growth.

In the complex scenario so far described, our proposal is to go back to Jane Jacobs' concept of import replacement and transfer it from the production of goods and services to the circulation, adoption, adaptation, diffusion of new and innovative ideas (of innovation). Indeed, one of Jacobs's chief insights is that import replacement leads to a diversification of available products for consumption and investment within a city and this brings positive impacts to local infrastructure and skills, therefore innovative capacity—not only production levels. Dealing with "old" things in new ways forges the path to doing completely new things never thought of before (Satell 2013). If "old" is assumed here as the import of an innovation in use elsewhere, it becomes clear that the engagement with the context is the key of the Jacobs' concept.

Looking at the larger and more open complexity of the contemporary cities, being aware of the networked nature of their interdependence and their inner dynamics, it is possible to reframe the import replacement concept making it more coherent with the concept of transition rather than the development one.

The two concepts of innovation scaling up and scaling out refer both mostly to the sphere of the innovation production system; in the first case it is related to the number of users or adopters, in the second to the change of the production system itself. The two concepts do not take into consideration the wider contexts and system where innovation is in action. The import replacement concept drives a reconceptualization of the two dynamics within a more systemic framework that takes into account that:

(1) the adoption of innovation does not depend uniquely on the quality and goodness of the innovation per se, as in the vision of den Ouden[2] (2012), rather it can be enabled, facilitated, pushed, sped up by the conditions of the urban context; it can be conceptualized more as an embedment process in which the context plays a relevant role;
(2) the process of scaling, in addition to the transformation of the innovation production system, can determine and contribute to the transformation of the context towards transition; it can therefore activate a process of synergy with other innovation spheres that ends up in value creation, networked and institutional learning, so affecting the regime level.

---

[2]"(...) if the [innovation] experience is pleasurable, it will also help the widespread adoption of the innovation (...)" (den Ouden 2012, p. 15).

In a pill, the Jacobs' concept of Import Replacement suggests a more systemic, context related view of innovation scaling up and scaling out, not privileging the product/service production system rather considering the urban ecosystem (including networks having here one or more active nodes). Scaling up assuming the meaning of context embedment and scaling out assumes the one of a contribution to transition processes.

3.4 Framing the Urbanscape

Although cities are generally considered relevant and rich environments for innovation to be ignited and developed, it is evident that cities can be differentiated for their proneness to innovation. From now on we define "Urbanscape" as the set of conditions making a city a prone or adverse environment towards innovation. Such conditions have been described under various concepts. Pelling et al. (2012) for example identify five 'drivers for adaptation towards change'; similarly, Kallis (2017), interpreting Norgaard (1994) talks about 'spheres of activities explaining co-evolution'. In both cases, drivers and spheres, the five elements are: technology, nature, values, knowledge, and institutions/social organisations. Harvey (2011) contributes to such a reflection identifying seven contributing factors: technological and organisational form, social relations, institutional and administrative arrangements, production and labour processes, relations to nature, the reproduction of daily life and of the species, and conceptions of the world.

Working on the overlapping meanings of spheres and factors while also considering the contribution by Landry (2008) in terms of the creative city, we have identified five dimensions as contributing factors to the city's proneness towards innovation: institutional capacity, cultural vibe, environmental awareness, social activism and integration, and entrepreneurial culture (Fig. 3.1).

In the authors' understandings, the five dimensions of the Urbanscape, are strongly related to the way a city manifests its proneness or its resistance to change;

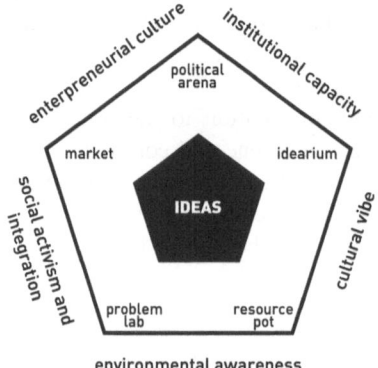

Fig. 3.1 The Urbanscape

3 Cities as Enablers of Innovation

they represent the enabling dynamics of the innovation capacity of the city. These enabling dynamics shape, orient, guide, activate the five interfaces described above as modes of interaction between the city and innovation processes. In a way, they shape the interactions between the regime and the niches. They have a precise, though complex, infrastructure that is in fact the regime as it is defined by Grin et al. (2010) and summarized in paragraph 3.2.1.

The Urbanscape is the result of the scape's interpretation made by the city as a complex system of actors and networks. It is a kind of *climate* of the city making it more or less comfortable for innovation processes (Fig. 3.2).

The Urbanscape intended as climate, results in the complex, rich and intense system of flows that any city represents and embodies; it embeds the dynamics of creativity in the city (the networks of flows that a city activates and is part of is also the key to its creativity). Florida (2000) with his idea of the creative class, and Landry (2008) with his creative city concept, have discussed and valued the role of creativity in socio-urban environments. It is with Gutzmer (2016) that the idea of city creativity is strongly related to the capacity of finding and creating new connections of, and consequently new operators' roles within, the network itself. It is through these dynamics that new knowledge is created.

> But this knowledge can no longer be understood as "rooted" in one superior source, it has its roots anywhere. There is no per-se knowing where knowledge might be created or where innovation might occur. For any actor who wants to find out where innovation might be generated in an urban setting, there is no alternative in the development of rather fine senses as the potential generation of newness in the urban field (Gutzmer 2016: 16).

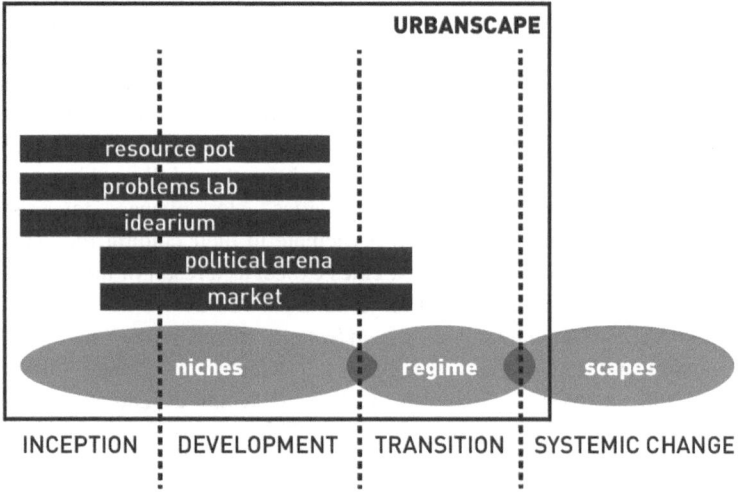

Fig. 3.2 Urban interfaces for innovation in the framework of the Urbanscape

A city's proneness towards innovation cannot be understood while disregarding urban knowledge, i.e. following existing knowledge flow networks and tracing active connections.

Institutional capacity is the ability of institutions to perform their functions. Over past decades, the concept has been often articulated in relation to that of governance, in particular to the governance model and structure used to perform such functions. According to Patsy Healey, institutional capacity deeply depends on the quality of local policy cultures. Some are well integrated, networked, and informed; usually they clearly reveal their sources of power and can easily activate internal and external resources. Others are fragmented, disconnected and do not work in a certain dynamic of power and knowledge (Healey 1998). Different governance models, i.e. different types of informal and formal partnerships, different networks and arenas involved and engaged in institutional functions, give rise to different abilities to cope with problems and changes. Although openness has recently become a relevant property of institutional capacity, the effectiveness of the openness is constrained by the institutions being able to coordinate and align a sound city identity and self-definition process; when a strong, clear and coordinated image of the city is lacking, no alignment of meanings and value is possible and any innovation risks being dispersed into the urban environment and it becomes hard or even impossible for innovation to be embedded in the fabric of a city.

Cities are stages for cultural activities that range from street art, underground music scenes, and diverse design, digital, audio, community and performative happenings as well as the well-known and more published cultural events and exhibitions. The intensity of such activities is the cities is an indicator of their cultural vibe. The *cultural vibe* of a city is defined by Montalto et al. (2017) as the cultural 'pulse' of a city in terms of cultural infra-structure and participation in culture (2017: 15). It is the output of the tangible and intangible assets which makes cities attract creative talent and stimulate cultural engagement: cultural life is a key element in a city's quality of life and a 'soft location factor' to attract talent; also participation in cultural activities increases people's networking among each other and with the place where they live, enhances their creative skills and improves their psychological well-being thus increasing cities' attractiveness towards local, national and international audiences to participate in their cultural life. This is the most basic and yet crucial outcome that cities expect as a result of their engagement in promoting arts and culture (Montalto et al. 2017: 16).

There is a growing phenomenon of *environmental awareness*: more and more people understand and defend the need to sustainably manage our planet's resources and ecosystems. Steven Cohen (Executive Director, Columbia University's Earth Institute in 2014)[3] wrote: "This has nothing to do with environmentalism or ideology. People, young people even more, know that we are

---

[3]Cohen S. (2015) *The Growing Level of Environmental Awareness.* A blog post: https://www.huffingtonpost.com/steven-cohen/the-growing-level-of-envi_b_6390054.html (accessed: December 2017).

stressing the planet's finite resources. This awareness, which could be considered a paradigm shift, is exerting pressure on many of the day-to-day actions routinely undertaken by corporations, government agencies and non-profits, along with behaviours seen in communities and households. Individual behaviour is changing as well". Cities contribute to widening this awareness when they engage, and are engaged by, citizens and companies in improving urban performances towards sustainability and, by doing this, activate collective experimental initiative for new knowledge production.

Learning is a social experience (Dewey 2007) and *social activism and integration* can be considered crucial learning experiences often taking place in urban environments. Defined as the attitude of taking an active part in events and movements, especially in social contexts, social activism and the need for integration are increasingly driving movement-like initiatives. Some scholarly works note the specific urban nature of contemporary social initiatives and activities. Shoene (2017) explored how urbanity and urban resources are predicting factors for citizens getting engaged in social activism and integration. Social activism and integration initiatives typically embed themselves in, and create, new networks in the cities and this is when and where "space of hopes" (Harvey 2000) are available. Uitermark et al. (2012) sustain that the city is constitutive of social movements, which are usually conflictual dynamics: density, size and diversity contribute to conflictual movement creation but diversity represents the opportunity for such movements to transform conflicts into opportunity for innovation.

To be creative, and possibly innovative in and for the city, companies have to behave in a network-like way, adding new links to the networks they interact with. Entering the urban sphere and becoming urban means to have the capacity to generate relations and infuse them into the urban network thus contributing to the city as a 'machine for learning' (McFarlane 2011). This explains why the urban sphere is such a focus point of innovative business strategy (Gutzmer 2016). The *entrepreneurial culture* of the city is consequently related to the way a city provides entrepreneurs (and innovation actors) with the opportunity to understand in a more complex and multidimensional way the connections and communication processes that drive its cultural as well as economic activity today.

Considering the Urbanscape, it is clear that innovation in the city is no longer something carried out in isolated laboratories; in the city, innovation agents can integrate their laboratories into a network of urban productivity. This is because cities are the environments where basic inputs are potentially transformed into elements of innovation, and eventually into new market reality. Any company or innovation actor isolated from any urban reality may find it difficult to sustain its innovation program, not only due to the market being concentrated into urban environments, but because of the isolation of the urban knowledge and relational networks (Gutzmer 2016).

To plug into the networks some creation of common meanings is necessary so that interactions become possible. It is in the urban field that diverse actors get together physically and create certain common grounds to guarantee meaningful interactions. Therefore, it is the cities which play this exact role: and the

Urbanscape enables the alignment of meanings[4] that represents the key to new relations and therefore to the creation of new knowledge.

References

Amin A, Thrift N (2002) Cities: reimagining the urban. Polity Press, Cambridge
Asheim B, Coenen L, Vang J (2007) Face-to-face, buzz, and knowledge bases: sociospatial implications for learning, innovation, and innovation policy. Env Plann C Polit Space 25 (5):655–670
Athey G, Nathan M, Webber C, Mahroum S (2008) Innovation and the city. Innov Organ Manag 10(2–3):156–169
Balducci A (2001) Trading Zone, un concetto utile per alcuni dilemmi dell'urbanistica. Crios 2:33–45
Cappellin R, Baravelli M, Bellandi M, Camagni R, Ciciotti R, Marelli E (2015) Investimenti, Innovazione e città. Una nuova politica industriale per la crescita. Egea, Milano
Castells M (1996) The information age: economy, society, and culture. Volume I: The rise of the network society. Blackwell Publishing, Oxford
Castells M (1997) The information age: economy, society and culture. The power of identity, vol 2. Blackwell Publishing, Oxford
Castells M (1998) The information age: economy, society and culture. End of millennium, vol 3. Blackwell Publishing, Oxford
Castells M (2001) Bausteine einer Theorie der Netzwerkgesellschaft. Berliner Journal für Soziologie 11(4):423–439
den Ouden E (2012) Innovation design. Creating value for people, organisations and society. Springer, London
Dewey J (2007) Experience and education. Simon and Schuster, New York
Duranton G, Puga D (2004) Micro-foundations of urban agglomeration economies. Handb Reg Urb Econ 4:2063–2117
Dvir T, Shamir B (2003) Follower developmental characteristics as predicting transformational leadership: a longitudinal field study. Lead Q 14:327–344
Dvir R, Pasher E (2004) Innovation engines for knowledge cities: an innovation ecology perspective. J Knowl Manag 8(5):16–27
Florida R (2000) Competing in the age of talent: environment, amenities, and the new economy. A report prepared for the R.K. Mellon Foundation, Heinz Endowments and Sustainable Pittsburgh
Grin J, Rotmans J, Schot, (2010) Transitions to sustainable development: new directions in the530 study of long term transformative change. Routledge, New York
Gutzmer A (2016) Urban innovation networks, understanding the city as a strategic resource. Springer International Publishing, Switzerland
Harvey D (2000) Spaces of hope. University of California Press
Harvey D (2011) The enigma of capital and the crises of capitalism. Profile Books
Healey P (1998) Building institutional capacity through collaborative approaches to urban planning. Env Plann A 30:1531–1546
Hirschman AO (1958) The strategy of economic development. Yale University Press, New Haven
Jacobs J (1969a) The life of cities. Random House
Jacobs J (1969b) The economy of cities. Vintage Books

---

[4]called *translations* by Tuomi, 2001.

Johnson B (2008) Cities, systems of innovation and economic development. Innov Manag Policy Pract 10(2–3):146–155

Kallis (2017) Economics without growth. In: Castells M (ed) Another economy is possible: culture and economy in a time of crisis. Polity Press, Cambridge

Kolb DA, Fry RE (1974) Toward an applied theory of experiential learning. MIT Alfred P. Sloan School of Management

Lambooy J (2010) The transmission of knowledge, emerging networks, and the role of universities: an evolutionary approach. Eur Plan Stud 12(5):643–657

Landry C (2008) The creative city: a toolkit for urban innovators. Earthscan, Canada

Leon N (2008) Attract and connect: the 22@Barcelona innovation district and the internationalisation of Barcelona business. Innovation 10(2–3):235–246

Martin R, Simmie J (2008) The theoretical bases of urban competitiveness: does proximity matter? In: Revue d'économie régionale et urbaine, Octobre: 333–351

McFarlane C (2011) The city as a machine for learning. Trans Inst Br Geogr 36:360–376

Mintzberg H (1985) The organisation as political arena. J Manag Stud 22(2):133–154

Montalto V, Tacao J, Moura C, Langedijk S, Saisana M (2017) The cultural and creative cities monitor. https://composite-indicators.jrc.ec.europa.eu/cultural-creative-cities-monitor/media/c3monitor2017.pdf. Accessed Nov 2017

Nelson M, Ehrenfeucht R (2016) Moving to safety? Opportunities to reduce vulnerability through relocation and resettlement policy. In: Brescia R, Marshall JT (eds) How cities will save the world: urban innovations in the face of population flows, climate change and economic equality. Routledge Press, New York, NY, pp 65–80

Norgaard RB (1994) Development betrayed: the end of progress and a coevolutionary revisioning of the future. Routledge

Pelling M, Manuel-Narravate D, Redclift M (2012) Climate change and the crisis of capitalism. In: Pelling M, Manuel-Narravate D, Redclift M (eds) Climate change and the crisis of capitalism. A change to reclaim self, society, and nature. Routledge, London, pp 1–18

Pinnegar S, Marceau J, Randolph B (2008) Innovation and technology challenges for the built environment industry. City Futures Research Centre, Issues Paper No 7, July

Pratt AC (2008) Creative cities: the cultural industries and the creative class. Geogr Ann 90(2):107–117

Reimer S, Pinch S, Sunley P (2008) Design spaces: agglomeration and creativity in British design agencies. Geografiska Annaler Ser B Hum Geogr 90:151–172

Rittel HWJ, Webber MM (1973) Dilemmas in a general theory of planning. Policy Sci 4(2):15–169

Satell G, How to manage innovation. On-line publication: https://www.forbes.com/sites/gregsatell/2013/03/07/how-to-manage-innovation-2/#544a3a5d4785, 2013

Schindler Sarah B (2016) Exploring OPTIONS for urban sustainability in an era of scarce water resources: a possible ban on lawns. In: Brescia R, Marshall JT (eds) How cities will save the world. Urban innovation in the face of population flows, climate change and economic inequality. Rutledge, pp 97–118

Schoene M (2017) Urban continent, urban activism? European cities and social movement activism. Glob Soc 31(3):370–391

Simmie J (2003) Innovative cities. Routledge

Stam E, De Jong JP, Marlet G (2008) Creative industries in the Netherlands: structure, development, innovativeness and effects on urban growth. Geografiska Annaler Ser B Hum Geogr 90:119–132

Stolarick K, Florida R (2006) Creativity, connections and innovation: a study of linkages in the Montréal Region. Env Plann A Econ Space 38(10):1799–1817

Straatemeier T, Bertolini L, te Brömmelstroet M, Hoetjes P (2010) An experiential approach to research, in planning. Env Plann B Urb Anal City Sci 37(4):578–591

Therrien P (2005) City and innovation: different size, different strategy. Eur Plan Stud 13(6):853–877

Uitermark J, Nicholls W, Loopmans M (2012) Cities and social movements. Theorizing beyond the right to the city. Env Plann A 44:2546–2554

Van Winden Willem (2014) Urban governance in the knowledge-based economy: challenges for different city types. Innovation 10(2–3):197–210

Wolfe DA, Bramwell A (2008) Innovation, creativity and governance: social dynamics of economic performance in city-regions. Innovation 10(2–3):170–182

Open Access This chapter is licensed under the terms of the Creative Commons Attribution 4.0 International License (http://creativecommons.org/licenses/by/4.0/), which permits use, sharing, adaptation, distribution and reproduction in any medium or format, as long as you give appropriate credit to the original author(s) and the source, provide a link to the Creative Commons license and indicate if changes were made.

The images or other third party material in this chapter are included in the chapter's Creative Commons license, unless indicated otherwise in a credit line to the material. If material is not included in the chapter's Creative Commons license and your intended use is not permitted by statutory regulation or exceeds the permitted use, you will need to obtain permission directly from the copyright holder.

Chapter 4
Innovation and Design

Grazia Concilio, Amalia De Götzen, Francesco Molinari,
Nicola Morelli, Ingrid Mulder, Luca Simeone, Ilaria Tosoni
and Kirsten Van Dam

4.1 Characterising Design Agency

4.1.1 Types of Design Agencies

As already highlighted in Chap. 3, design is about creating value for users through specific activities. However, value creation activities can be very different and can involve different actors in relation to the specific context in which the design action takes place. In the old industrial production perspective, the focus was on the production process where value was created, with a clear distinction between production and use phase. In this perspective, the value creation process was independent from its context. This is still true when services are considered in a product dominant logic, where users are (passively) served by the service personnel, who are fully in charge of the service quality. The responsibility for the design and the value creation process of such service is mostly, if not entirely, in the hands of the service provider.

However, within business, marketing, communication and design studies, the last decades have seen a substantial shift from a product-centric perspective to a perspective which focuses on the interaction between the consumer and the service context (Service Dominant logic), in which value is defined by and co-created with

---

G. Concilio · I. Tosoni
Politecnico di Milano, Milan, Italy

A. De Götzen · N. Morelli (✉) · L. Simeone · K. Van Dam
Aalborg University, Aalborg, Denmark
e-mail: nmor@create.aau.dk

F. Molinari
Anci Toscana, Florence, Italy

I. Mulder
Technische Universiteit Delft, Delft, The Netherlands

© The Author(s) 2019
G. Concilio and I. Tosoni (eds.), *Innovation Capacity and the City*,
PoliMI SpringerBriefs, https://doi.org/10.1007/978-3-030-00123-0_4

the consumer, rather than embedded in output (Vargo and Lusch 2004: 6). The fundamental change in this approach is illustrated by the Vargo and Lusch statement that the enterprise cannot deliver value, but only offers value propositions, which means it cannot create and/or deliver value independently (Vargo and Lusch 2008).

Along a similar line of thinking, Normann and Ramirez (1994) shift the focus of the value creation activity from the production phase, to the use phase. The co-production of value is manifested in the offer to which several actors contribute by performing specific activities; the offer is, therefore, the result of myriad activities performed by many people dispersed throughout time and space. Assets and resources (material objects, technologies, knowledge) available in an offer are combined in a systematic way thus ensuring access for users. Ultimately, whether customers buy a product or a 'service', they are really buying access to resources (Ibid.: 48). Normann and Ramirez use the case of IKEA to explain the way users can be considered as an active and crucial part of the value production process.

This perspective of design, strictly related to value creation processes, enriches the recurrent definition of design coming from the work of Herbert Simon, who describes design as "[devising] courses of action aimed at changing existing situations into preferred ones" (Simon 1969/1982: 129). This definition reflects a vision where the design process is articulated into two distinct phases of planning ("devising courses of action") and implementation ("changing existing situations into preferred ones"). Operationally, design can be seen as an everyday problem-solving capability. Ezio Manzini labels this capability as *diffuse design*. In his words, design is the outcome of combining three human gifts:

> Critical sense (the ability to look at the state of things and recognize what cannot, or should not be, acceptable), creativity (the ability to imagine something that does not yet exist), and practical sense (the ability to recognize feasible ways of getting things to happen). Integrating the three makes it possible to imagine something that is not there, but which could be if appropriate actions were taken (Manzini 2015: 31).

Design, the process through which possibilities are consciously created (Metcalf 2014: vii), is a "natural capacity" (Manzini 2015: 47) that is largely diffused and that is widely applied to solve everyday problems. Besides being oriented toward problem-solving, design—the very activity of devising and testing courses of action—also helps in framing problems and, more generally, making sense of things (Manzini 2015; Krippendorff 2006, Schön 1987).[1]

While diffuse design is a general human capacity and activity, some people study and practice design at an expert level. This is what Manzini refers to as *expert design* and this is how he introduces it:

---

[1]Along this line of thinking, Donald Schön's idea of design as a process where doing and thinking are complementary has been influential. Schön states that "doing extends thinking in the tests, moves, and probes of experimental action, and reflection feeds on doing it and its results. Each feeds the other, and each sets boundaries for the other" (Schön 1987: 280).

> Let's start with the following statement: every human talent may evolve into a skill and sometimes into a discipline (meaning a culture, tools, and professional practice): everybody can run, but not everybody takes part in the marathon and few become professional athletes; everybody can tap out the beat with a tambourine, but not everybody plays in a group and few make a living playing it professionally. Similarly, everybody is endowed with the ability to design, but not everybody is a competent designer and few become professional designers (Manzini 2015: 37).

The relevance and functioning of *diffuse design* agency is shown by several pieces of evidence. Among them, the most important are related to the growing number of people who, pushed by the global financial crisis of 2008–2013, have engaged in innovative activities, or what Castells and Hlebik (in Castells et al. 2017) define as alternative economics practices. These are related to production, consumption, exchange, payment, and credit. They are all to be intended as innovative and at the same time viable alternatives to solve problems that global challenges create with regards to everyday life. In fact, it is in daily life that diffuse design competences appear with their operational capacity: by imagining, shaping and creating alternative local futures in which they can live *with* rather than *against*.

Expert design emerges from the work of design professionals, "of those subjects whose field of interest, of research, and ultimately of work is the practice and culture of design" (Manzini 2015: 1).

The characterisation of diffuse and expert design makes design a practical problem-solving epistemology (Metcalf 2014: 92), a necessary human capacity (Bánáthy 1996; Cross 2011). It builds upon a purposeful polarisation. As Manzini also states:

> These two poles with their corresponding profiles are an abstraction: what interests us is the extent of the field of possibility they indicate, the infinite variations that may appear within them, and especially their sociocultural dynamics (Manzini 2015: 37).

Within the framework described in Chap. 3, and within the four different dynamics that are there described (transformation, de-alignment and re-alignment, technological substitution and reconfiguration pathway), we can identify different design agencies, both human and non-human.

Table 4.1 captures the nuances of design processes that might be not only driven by human agencies (e.g., diffuse or expert design), but can also be affected by other agencies, i.e. socio-technical, institutional or cultural factors. The table details how, within the Service Dominant logic, users (or customers, or citizens) actively select and aggregate resources according to their wants and needs; it summarises some key elements that allow us to characterise human and non-human design agency while taking into account the prevailing activity of design related to value creation. In the table diffuse and expert design are identified as human design agencies and are described through the capabilities and roles they can play; also, regime and scape are identified as design agencies due to their contextual influence and role in shaping conditions for design activities and opportunities. Considering scape and regime as "design agencies", in fact, allows us to take into consideration the fact that design processes are affected by the social, economic, technologic and cultural

Table 4.1 Characterisation of design agency

Type of agent	Design agency	Characterization
Human	Diffuse design	Design as the inherent individual capabilities to generate new solutions. This builds upon the notion of diffuse design as general human capacity and activity. Users select and aggregate resources in light of their wants and needs (e.g., through processes of mediation, interpretation and articulation —Björgvinsson et al. 2012)
	Expert design	Expert design emerges from the work of design professionals, "of those subjects whose field of interest, of research, and ultimately of work is the practice and culture of design" (Manzini 2015: 1). These subjects are well versed in the use of design approaches and tools and they have a design knowledge that allows them to maintain a critical and constructive attitude. Expert design generates infrastructures (e.g., products/services) for value creation. This is also the way in which expert design triggers diffuse design. This happens when users aggregate resources that come already pre-structured (by expert designers) in form of products and/ or services (e.g., through processes such as adaptation, appropriation, tailoring, re-design, and maintenance— Björgvinsson et al. 2012)
Non-human	Scape as a designer	The cultural, economic, and societal paradigmatic framework which, when experiencing crises, may activate change processes. The scape is an unintentional designer.
	Regime as a designer	The social, economic, technologic and cultural context— expressed through institutional structures (e.g., authorities, law, the marketplace)—creates frameworks that influence the design activity, often shaping design principles and specifications. The regime is a (more or less aware) intentional designer

contexts in which they unfold. As non-human agencies expressed through institutional structures (e.g., authorities, law, the marketplace), they create frameworks which influence the design activity at various degrees of intensity, oftentimes even affecting the very definition of design principles and specifications.

Both diffuse and expert design work as enablers at different stages of the change process and at different levels of the socio-technical structures—from localised and context-anchored projects to projects which specifically frame the embedding of the design product into the social and political realm; they act either in niches or in regimes.

> **Stories of diffuse and expert design**
> **#1 Diffuse design**
> DIY design-driven movements. WikiBlock is an open-source library for DIY urban furniture which enables everyone to become an urban designer. Frustrated by his own neighbourhood, the founder of Wikiblock was triggered to change it and looked for ways to revitalise lifeless urban areas and help neighbourhoods and communities. The open-source library WikiBlock therefore offers a wide selection of urban furniture. Benches, chairs, planters, mini stages, beer garden fences, kiosks—only, they are not for sale. Users and citizens can select and design and make it by themselves, depending on their own needs and wishes. Designs, construction plans and files can be downloaded for free. Taken to a local CNC workshop, the individual parts can be simply whipped out of plywood. Just like an ordinary IKEA product, the components can be easily assembled without the use of glue, nails or complex tools.
> **#2 Expert design**
> Within the IKEA system the value (a furnished home) is in fact created by users, who imagine how to furnish their home, measure their home space, visit IKEA, pick up and transport the disassembled furniture and mount it. However IKEA supported the value creation process by designing every aspect from the service to support this value creation process, from the catalogue (pictures of different home interiors help non-expert users to figure out how the space is shaped by different pieces of furniture, materials and colours), to the structure of the furniture items (that are disassembled and can easily be reassembled) to the exhibition, in which, after leaving the kids to play in the playground, customers can test the furniture (they can sit on a sofa/chair), figure out how they fit in suggested home interiors, pick up what they need in compact and transportable packages and read the assembly instructions.

Diffuse design can be characterized as an activity of selecting and aggregating resources to change existing situations into preferred ones (Simon 1969/1982). Users look at existing resources from their own viewpoint, pull resources from various sources and aggregate these resources in light of their specific problems, needs or wants (through processes of interpretation, mediation and articulation). This activity of aggregating and integrating existing resources is part of everyday life, it may concern the decisions about the most common and repetitive actions (which mostly rely on standard procedures and conventional ways of aggregating resources, for example the everyday commuting activity to work) or may refer to the solution of crucial individual or social problems that require a creative effort to generate new aggregations, also using new tools and infrastructure. For example (referred to a niches scale), in the DIY movement, users can get their own 3D printer (or build it using open hardware and open source software components), download some 3D renders from Internet (e.g., licensed as Creative Commons objects) and create their own product, for example a series of custom-made action figures representing a new species of aliens. Users aggregate existing resources to create something—the 3D-printed action figures—meaningful for them. Another example (referred to the regime scale) comes from the alderman of Milan in charge of sport activities and infrastructure. In order to respond to the growing request for free public spaces by practitioners of new urban sports (parkour, skating…) the alderman has implemented an existing procedure (for the temporary use of public land) available for private actors, as to have the right to assign specific spaces for free without compelling the users to pay for them. A new aggregation of existing resources made on the basis of daily life experience at the regime level and without the specific intervention of a design expert.

Expert design unfolds through the description of a change, through the production of a blueprint and the plan of future visions. It is based on technical competences and it is domain specific. It creates the structure in which value creation can happen. Expert designers are well versed in the use of design approaches and tools and have a design knowledge that allows them to maintain a critical and constructive/creative attitude. While framing problems and devising courses of actions, design experts can rely upon their experience and refer, for example, to repertoires of already developed design projects, to guidelines, heuristics, criticism.

Our framework of design agencies—in particular, the two categories of human and non-human and their additional articulation into diffuse/expert design and scape/regime as designer—require further articulation of the notion of design thinking. Design thinking posits itself as a critique of traditional, hyper-rational ways of problem solving. In contrast to analytic thinking, it puts openness and a radical focus on creativity at the centre of business productivity.

Considering the diverse design agencies, it is clear that there is no single design thinking, there is no single way of thinking in a designer-like way. Rather, different forms of design thinking can be connected to different types of design agencies:

- In *diffuse* design, design thinking can be seen as the general human capacity to look at the state of things and recognise what cannot, or should not, be acceptable, to imagine something that does not exist yet and to recognise feasible ways of getting things to happen (Manzini 2015). It is worth noticing that this capacity does not include specific design methodologies, but rather employs intrinsic cognitive resources.
- In *expert* design, specific design methods and design knowledge (e.g., repertoires of already developed design projects, guidelines, heuristics, criticism) help in identifying and framing problems and proposing solutions. Here design thinking is anchored to the practice and the culture of design professionals. Design methods and approaches can enhance the general human skills related to diffuse design and provide a specific way of looking at the state of things, of imagining and deploying new courses of actions.

As also illustrated in Table 4.1, different types of design agencies emerge from wider contexts at the level of scapes and regimes. This has also an impact on the characterization of design thinking, which in both forms is influenced by:

- *Scapes* as sort of meta designers: by crises that affect a scape (see Chap. 3) different change processes are activated that require design actions at different levels. Design thinking in this case is related to the creation of evidences at global cultural and ideological reflexive level that novelties are needed to deal and tackle with the causes of the scape crises; regime and niches then are activated.
- The conditions of *regimes*: solicited by crises in the scape, regime is in charge of the creation of conditions at the level of niches to produce novelties as well as of the re-shaping of the regime structures, functions, roles and goals.

Design thinking at the level of diffuse and expert design operates in a way that both affects and is affected by specific conditions of scapes, regimes and niches.

4.1.2 The Infrastructuring Role of the Design Agency

Individuals create value by aggregating resources. The term infrastructuring can describe the expert design intervention in resource aggregation -and therefore in value-creation. There are two ways to aggregate resources:

- the first is related to the production of novel solutions the interpretation, adoption and use of which represent the value creation moment; for example, people use their diffuse design capability to aggregate and/or re-adapt existing products or services to address their needs: people organise spontaneous car sharing initiatives or solidarity purchasing groups, thus aggregating existing resources (cars, booking systems, online groups on social networks) into new solutions. In respect to this way of aggregating resources, infrastructuring happens when an expert designer supports diffuse design by triggering, inspiring or facilitating people's creativity, or engaging them in value co-creation.
- the second way of creating resources is related to the production of products and services which create conditions for value to be generated. In this case the activity of infrastructuring includes the most common design activities, consisting in aggregating technical knowledge, professional experience, existing products and technologies, to generate products and services which users will use to produce value that addresses their own needs. In operative terms, infrastructuring refers to "a priori" activities: selection, design, development and deployment of resources.

Infrastructure may also consist of digital platforms, physical spaces, public innovation spaces, information and logistic services (Manzini 2015) which support an ongoing alignment between contexts, cultures, attitudes and routines and the interaction among the several actors involved (including customers). In this sense, infrastructure is also related to activities of mediation, interpretation and further articulation of resources as proposed by Björgvinsson et al. (2010). According to this perspective, coherent with the Service Dominant Logic, designers propose the interface or the contextual conditions for the interaction to happen, and design the infrastructure, i.e. the processes supporting the interaction (Secomandi and Snelders 2011), but they cannot exactly control the outcome of the interaction happening through, as it happen in several services, in which value is essentially created by customers.

While the activity in the value-creation phase aims at facilitating or supporting interaction, the activity of expert designers, that create the ground for the interaction is often based on a more "traditional" planning activity, which includes the analysis of the context, the definition of blueprints, the coordination of time sequences and technological infrastructures and the design of products. Platforms such as Amazon.com or eBay or Netflix derive from the work of expert designers but their value emerges only when the final users perform operations such as creating and sharing personal lists, curating and maintaining personal repositories, creating personalized distribution channels, etc. It is through these operations that value emerges when the users adapt, appropriate and tailor these platforms in light of their own needs and wants.

Within the broad design field, a good number of scholars and practitioners have framed their design activities in terms of creating and maintaining 'infrastructures' for collaboration (Binder et al. 2011; Björgvinsson et al. 2012; Ehn et al. 2014; Le Dantec and Di Salvo 2013; Star and Bowker 2002; Simeone 2016). An infrastructure can be a physical space where various stakeholders (e.g., government officials, companies, citizens) are invited to participate in sessions where problems of common interest are defined and where solutions are imagined, tested and implemented. For example, a physical space containing equipment such as laser cutters, 3D printers, CNC milling machines and other tools (such as a FabLab or other kinds of makerspaces or innovation spaces) can be considered as an open infrastructure which can host various people and organisations interested in developing and prototyping their ideas, concepts for new products or services, social and cultural interventions. Such infrastructure could, for example, host a hackathon where various stakeholders are involved in exploring issues of common interest and, together, contribute to frame problems and prototype possible solutions. An infrastructure does not necessarily need a physical space, though. Thematically-linked participatory sessions can be organised in multiple spaces (Binder et al. 2011), for example using the premises of the various stakeholders involved and/or through a series of interlinked participatory activities to be carried out via Internet. An infrastructure could also be a logical space for interaction, this is the case of interaction platforms for social networking (in which users create value by exchanging knowledge, ideas or their own feelings) or for mutual value exchange (where users create value by offering or receiving hospitality, car lifts, used objects). Within design research, projects based upon infrastructure have been extensively carried out and analysed, particularly as a way in which to work with different and multiple stakeholders (Karasti 2014; Star and Bowker 2002; Star and

Ruhleder 1996; Le Dantec and Di Salvo 2013; Hillgren et al. 2011, 2013; Lukens 2013).

In particular, the characterisation of design agencies as distributed across diffuse design and expert design allows for the infrastructuring process to be articulated into two approaches:

- The *consultant* approach. In this approach, expert designers generate new formal structures (i.e., products/services platforms) for value creation. These structures can support changes within niches or regime. An example of this approach is crowdfunding services and platforms, such as Indiegogo (www.indiegogo.com) and Kickstarter (www.kickstarter.com). Kickstarter started as a service where independent artists, filmmakers, tinkerers, and entrepreneurs could raise money for worthwhile ideas, but has changed from fundraising crowd-based financing to community building. Within this approach, although focussed on the "energy" of the crowd, the value creation process is exclusively based on expert design.
- The *activist* approach. In this approach, diffuse design is ignited and sustained through infrastructures for collaboration. An example of this approach is a project called Precious Plastics, which is a design for a recycling centre of open source machines, tools and infrastructures (a collaborative platform) to fight *plastic* pollution from the bottom up. It is open source and supports people's own capability to recycle factories and further develop the design (www.preciousplastic.com).

4.2 A 3D Design-Based Innovation Space

Starting from the seminal work of Verganti (2009), design driven innovation can be defined as a process of value production, creation, and development that adds radically new meanings to current functions (incremental innovation) or to new and possibly disruptive functions (radical innovation).

In his discourse, Verganti mostly refers to innovation in the industrial design field, and the examples he makes are mainly related to products (objects, however complex), which have been successful in the consumer market.

An implicit assumption of Verganti's work seems to be that the definition of design is limited to the valuable ability of skilled and creative people, those that in daily life are called designers by profession, to expert designers. It is mostly due to their initiative, and to the success of their value propositions within the consumers (specifically) or customers (more generally), that new and radical meanings are added, perceived, and developed. According to this vision, designers act as a kind of interpreter: of popular values, environmental contexts, and collective needs. And design-driven innovation is a process (or strategy, as the figure above is labelled) delivering its outputs in the creation, integration, and production of value (through the radical change of meanings).

Therefore, according to Verganti, the value added by design to innovation continues to enable the radical change of meaning and the related value system. In many examples from Verganti's book, innovation derives from the integration of a product's functional value (capacity to respond to a need) with other sources of value such as emotion, fitness, etc.

However, in his discourse, technology is also relevant and, along with meaning, defines the space of innovation as two-dimensional, like in the figure above.

The above representation suggests an important consideration: despite the fact that design is strictly and uniquely related to radical changes in meaning, its role can be as important for incremental innovation as it is for radical innovation. If for instance, we think of the traditional (old fashioned but still valid) definition of design, as the "Purpose or planning that exists behind an action, fact, or object" (Oxford dictionary), design is the ability that allows anybody to envision a new artefact (be it a fork, a service or an entire city) and to plan how to make it. This can also be applicable to incremental innovation examples, where the role of design, although still interpretative, can be more limited, purely technical, or problem solving related.

This view on the design activity is not considered in Verganti's perspective, which instead focuses on the activity carried out by creative and skilled professional, rather than on the design activity suggested above. No doubt creativity is crucial for design: this is a shared idea among scientists exploring ways and conditions to push innovation. A recent article exploring statistics of creative jobs and positions in public and private organisations assigns a critical value to creativity in design for innovation (Dvir and Pasher 2004). Still designers are not only skilled professionals—or no longer so. We are familiar with more and more cases where interpreters of contexts and/or creators of new meanings are ordinary people (Castells 2017), not just designers, who collaboratively work together with the technical or domain experts to generate innovation.

In conclusion we can say that innovation and design are strictly connected: innovation, either incremental or radical, needs design! To make room for this statement, we added a third dimension to Verganti's model of design driven innovation in Fig. 4.1. This dimension focuses on the design competences, drawing the distinction—for us, crucial—between "expert" and "diffuse" design (Fig. 4.2), while still keeping the value assigned by Verganti to the dynamics of meaning and value creation.

By so doing, alongside the contribution of technical experts, as in the traditional design concept, we will consider the role of creative people as well as the making of complex, distributed, interactive environments of crowdsourced creativity: a collective mind of creators (Castells 2017), the diffuse design agency. Introducing diffuse design as a relevant innovation factor implies that we capture opportunities for co-creation and co-creativity within the networks which are active or potentially activated in a specific context. In this view Design becomes a tool with which to envision the innovative potential to change practices and behaviours through new products, services, and platforms.

4 Innovation and Design

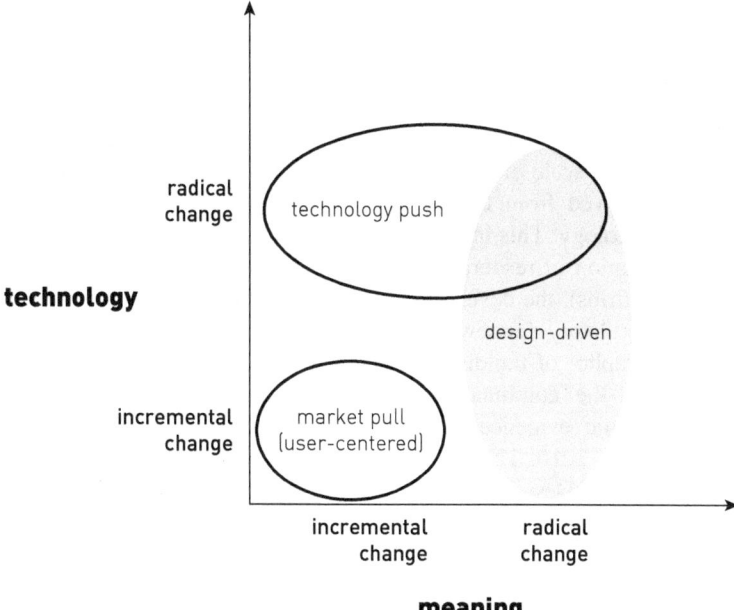

Fig. 4.1 Verganti's model of design-driven innovation (2009)

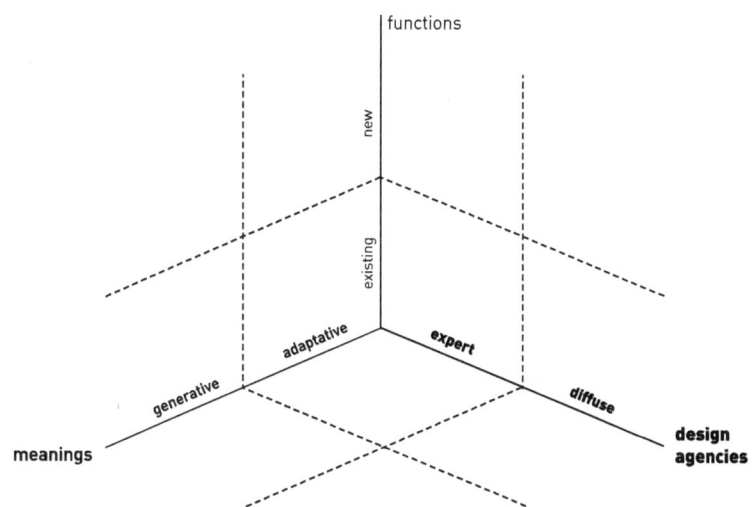

Fig. 4.2 The 3D innovation space

This model, by focussing on functions rather than on technologies, considers that technological change has an incessant, endogenous, dynamic in modern societies. It reduces, though not abolish, the role of technology in being the prime movers in innovation processes and adds in the role of change agency as assigning actors an equally important role in defining innovation paths (Grin et al. 2010: 13). This is not only true at the scale of niches but also at that of regime. The socio-technical perspective borrowed from Grin et al. (2010) is based on a contextual understanding of technology. This implies the creation of knowledge and prototypes, but also the mobilization of resources, the creation of social networks (e.g. sponsors, potential users, firms), the development of visions, the construction of markets, as well as new regulatory frameworks. Hughes (1986, quoted in Grin et al 2010) adopted the metaphor of building a "seamless web", to signify that technological change requires the combination of physical artefacts, organisations, natural resources, scientific evidences as well as legislative artefacts and governance models (Grin et al. 2010: 12)

The 3D model of Design Enabled Innovation is based on two persuasions. The first considers there to be no innovation without design: however generative or adaptive the production of meanings may be, design keeps its innovation-enabling role by combining meanings with existing or new functions in order to develop conditions for value creation. This persuasion considers that many design activities take place in and for innovation, but we tend to ignore it when innovation is not disruptive or when its ability to conquer a wide large market is weak. When the creation of novelties does not achieve a large success, it is not due to the lack of design work in it rather for the huge, uncontrolled uncertainty and for the large amount of unpredictable factors. It is not possible to assert that design is involved only when innovation achieves a successful scale without incurring in a logical mistake of its definition.

The second persuasion takes into account what has been discussed in the previous paragraph: creativity is not (only) an extraordinary moment of an exceptional break-out but a "way of life". Creativity can be considered the current practice for millions of people: it includes survival strategies, copying, pasting and adding activities, enacted by students across the world, and even the remix approach to music creation. Creativity is a surprising resource of the "crowd" considered in terms of its ability to produce new knowledge and new meanings with and for the cognitive, information and practice networks (Castells 2017). The concept of diffuse design embodies the networking ability of individuals and their potential creative contribution to innovation inside the networked structure of society. See the following URL: https://designscapes.eu/city-snapshots/ for a mapping exercise of several innovation examples.

In this 3D model some known forms of innovation can be represented that articulate the space (Fig. 4.3).

As already discussed, Verganti's book does not clearly state that design-driven innovation is exclusively referred to design professionals but the several examples he produces, all coming from the industrial design domain, are referred to design activities by professionals (Fig. 4.4).

4 Innovation and Design

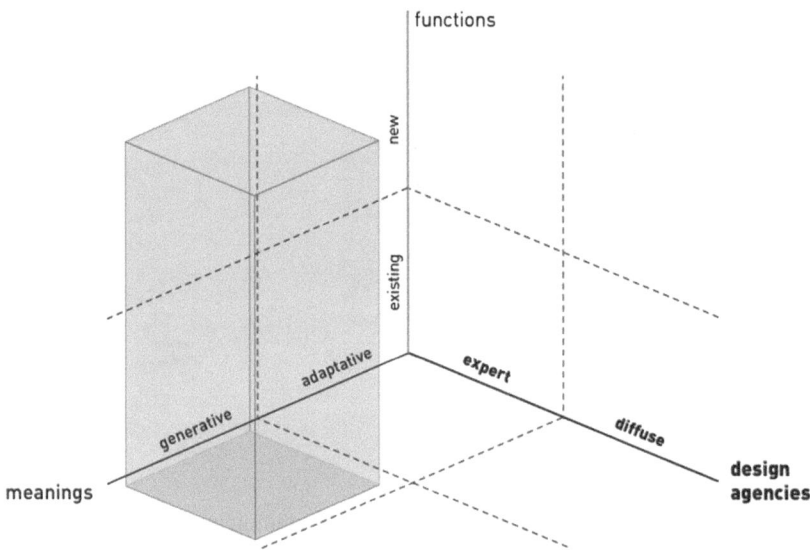

Fig. 4.3 Verganti's design driven 3D innovation space

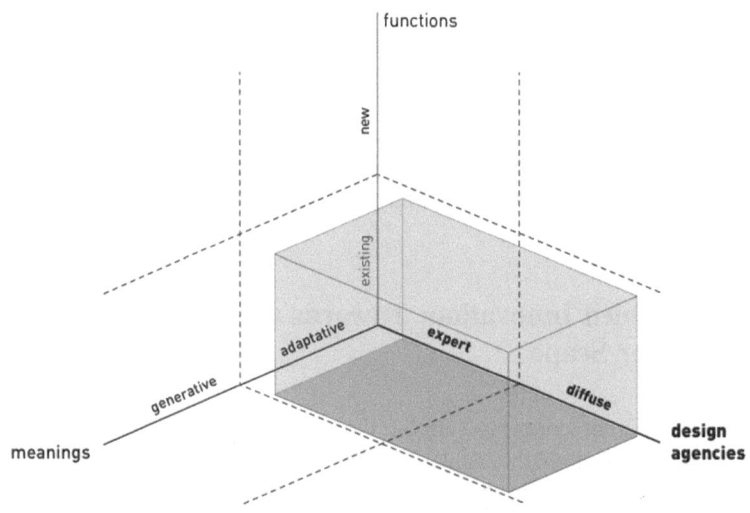

Fig. 4.4 Incremental 3D innovation space

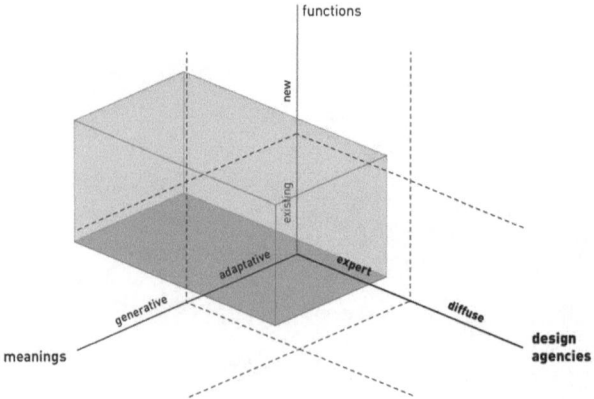

Fig. 4.5 Disruptive 3D innovation space

Incremental innovation is the one that clearly contemplates the role of diffuse design. This is possible for two reasons: everyday life problem solving and design capacity are easily activated/adopted by already existing "functions" and combined with and adaptive development of meanings (Fig. 4.5).

Some writers use open and disruptive innovation in an ambiguous way. Looking at the 3D space we consider that open innovation can be supportive of disruptive innovation but it does not guarantee its occurrence. The openness in fact guarantees the introduction of potential innovation forces which may in turn introduce opportunities for innovation to be disruptive. Such innovation forces do not only contemplate expert design but also diffuse design agencies (Fig. 4.6).

The 3D model of Design Enabled Innovation will be used in the next chapter in order to represent innovation processes throughout different maturity levels.

4.3 Design Enabled Innovation: Towards the Notion of Design for Scape

In the literature, different concepts support the understanding of the interplay between design and innovation, thus underlying their reciprocity. This reciprocity is not only evident in the academic discussion but also in several public initiatives promoting design adoption in companies and institutions for guiding and supporting innovation (Table 4.2).

Various design agencies—diffuse design, expert design—support innovation across the different levels of innovation maturity (ignition, development, transition towards systemic change). Different design goals correspond to each innovation maturity level, as shown in the Table 4.3.

Diffuse design and expert design can support the preliminary activities of discovering opportunities and challenges, generating ideas and developing and testing.

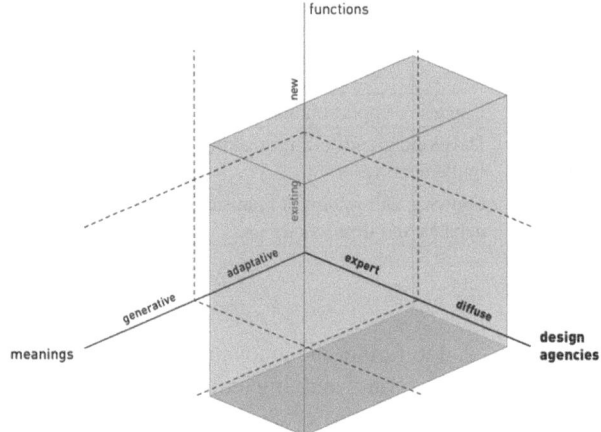

Fig. 4.6 Open 3D innovation space

Table 4.2 Design and innovation in combined definitions

Design for user-centred innovation	Design for user-centred innovation is the activity of conceiving and developing a plan for a new or significantly improved product, service or system which ensures the best interface with user needs, aspirations and abilities, and which allows for aspects of economic, social and environmental sustainability to be taken into account[a]
Design and open innovation	Chesbrough (2003) introduced open innovation and described it in this manner: "open innovation is a paradigm which assumes that firms can and should use external ideas as well as internal ideas, and internal and external paths to the market, as the firms look to advance their technology." In fact, open innovation is the flow of knowledge, information and collaboration which helps accelerate design, innovation, creating value and sustainability
Design-driven innovation	Design-driven innovation is defined in this way: "Design-driven innovation is an approach to innovation based on the observation that people do not just purchase products, or services, they buy 'meaning'—where users' needs are not only satisfied by form and function, but also through experience (meaning)[b]
Business models design	A business model is a strategy or plan which has to not only create value but also capture the value in a meaningful way so that it can beat or compete with other ideas, methods, products, services, things, items, processes, tools or technology as well as capture unmet needs and opportunities in the market (Chesbrough 2007). The function of a business model includes: value proposition, value creation, market segment, the structure of the value chain, revenue generation/return on investment, cost structure, its network value, key partners, activities, channels, competitive strategy to find potential collaborators, alliances, joint ventures and competitors

[a]EC Staff Working Document, 2009, Design a driver of user-centred innovation. http://ec.europa.eu/DocsRoom/documents/2583/attachments/1/translations/en/renditions/native
The Commission Staff Working Document (2013) states that: "user-centred design thinking drives business model innovation, organisational innovation and other forms of non-technological innovation"
[b]http://www.designforeurope.eu/what-design-driven-innovation

Table 4.3 Linking design-centred activities with levels of innovation maturity

Levels of innovation maturity	Design goals
Inception	Capturing opportunities and challenges; generating ideas
Development	Developing and testing; making the case; delivering and implementing
Transition	Growing and scaling, organisational setting, activating public debates and discussions

Expert design is then needed to further the innovation process through the activities of making the case and delivering and implementing. Finally, the perspective offered when design operates in a broader context helps for the activities to grow, scale and ensure their organisational adaptation/adjustment.

The different agencies of design could be exemplified by a case of local, insurgent innovation, started as a spontaneous aggregation of a group of citizens:

> **STORY #3 The waste oil collection**
>
> No residential collection for organic oil waste is carried out in Milan by the waste management agency. Still the organic oil waste has to be conveyed to dedicated waste collection centres in the city. In order to reduce the number of conferring activities, one family starts collecting organic oil waste in a bottle to be conferred less frequently. During a condominium meeting, the family suggests the collection be made for the condominium and a common decision is made to have a 5-liter pot used for oil collection. When the pot is full and one of the residents in the condominium goes to the waste collection centres, the pot is emptied and brought back and the cycle starts again. A small, local change which represents an innovation epiphany is achieved. This small, local change is fostered by diffuse design in the form of the ability of this group of families inhabiting this condominium to identify problems, generate ideas and prototype a solution.
>
> A further step could be made, for example, when one of the inhabitants of the condominium—a design student in her fourth year—thinks that she could offer this service to other buildings of the area. She then talks to a couple of fellow students at her university and together they carry out some preliminary user research to check whether their idea can be of interest, they brainstorm on possible ideas and solutions ("Should we buy a cargo bike? Or a used small truck?"), they elaborate service walkthroughs and blueprints and, finally, they decide to try out their offering. To do this, they could organise the first condominium as an initial prototype and later on represent and communicate the concept to other buildings, in order to transfer it. They create a website where buildings and families can schedule services related to organic oil collection and disposal. They also prepare some flyers and a Facebook page to advertise their service. Way of

thinking and methods of expert design helped these students to get their idea off the ground.

After a few months, things go well to a point that they are able to expand a bit and serve about 100 buildings in their neighbourhood. At this macro level, things are much more complex. They need a different perspective that takes into consideration organisational, logistics and economic factors. They need to take into consideration potential regulations in the city, look for emerging competitors, deal with administrative authorizations. Perhaps, they need to think how they can differentiate and further expand their offering ("Should we also have a dedicated service for restaurants? Can we propose our service to other cities?"). The broader view of design for scapes here is helpful in order to operate at the level of complex systems of cities and beyond. At this level, the initial idea of this group of students needs to be systematically organised and communicated to the municipal authorities, in order to scale up the service to a broader urban scale.

The table below provides a summary on how design agencies can support various innovation activities in the *Waste Collection* story illustrated in the above box, which is mapped onto the three levels of innovation maturity (Table 4.4).

As a further articulation of the above discussion, we distinguish various dimensions of innovation in relation to the impact achieved:

Table 4.4 How design agencies can support various innovation activities

Innovation maturity level	Situation described in the waste oil case	Diffuse design	Expert design
Inception	"I don't want to be bothered". Citizens in the condominium find it problematic to take the used organic oil to the deposit	General human ability to look at the state of things and recognize what cannot, or should not, be acceptable (Manzini 2015)	Discovering and framing the problem (e.g., through user research based upon ethnographic observations, interviews, etc.)
	"We put a container in the basement" Someone comes out with a solution	General human ability to imagine something that does not exist yet (Manzini 2015)	Generating ideas through methods such as scenarios, creative techniques, brainstorming sessions, participatory design

(continued)

Table 4.4 (continued)

Innovation maturity level	Situation described in the waste oil case	Diffuse design	Expert design
Development	"Let's try it" A small "prototype" is created, to check how the idea works	General human ability to recognise feasible ways of getting things to happen (Manzini 2015)	Prototyping or developing through methods such as service walkthrough, business model canvas, etc
	The service is thoroughly assessed in the context of its use	Testing in daily life and assessing	Creating proofs of concept
	The service is organized at a level that can be fully operationally deployed	Small local adaptations in service adoption	Using a design approach for final delivery by, for example, organising, blueprinting and managing implementation processes
Transition	The service offer expands to other buildings, to other cities, to other waste materials towards more aware behaviours and practices	Adaptation to a broader scale with regards to service adoption	Design multiple dimensions by mapping the specific system and the stakeholders, by supporting the creation of the ecosystem and transferring the concepts to other contexts and to other products by taking into consideration organisational, economic, cultural and social implications for scaling up to complex systems of cities and beyond, behavioural change, communication

- Local—at this level innovation can be insurgent i.e. pushed by problems experienced by individuals in daily life, which are drivers of a change as a modification of current conditions towards an improvement;
- Structured—at this level innovation is guaranteed by a dedicated design activity which is necessary to create a structure for the idea to be prototyped, tested and implemented; the innovation achieves a change which is substantial at a local scale (the development scale in the niches) but does not reach the regime;

- Eco-systemic—at this level innovation is guaranteed by an important and long-lasting design strategy; the innovation achieves a change which is radical at the regime scale.

The discussion carried out up to this point has focused on the enabling role of design in innovative processes as an activity that is able to target value creation. As described in Chap. 3 (mainly quoting den Ouden 2012), it is crucial that innovation processes are able to target value creation at different levels of a socio-technical system at the same time. Using the categories addressed by den Ouden, design should work simultaneously for value creation at the level of users, of organisations, of the ecosystem and of Society. The role of Society in den Ouden's discussion is clearly described as the mass payer of the global problems' costs i.e. the owner of the current global societal challenges. In some sense society is the operational, daily life, touch point of the landscape. Her idea is that the urgency in the current global situation for societal challenges to find a response requires innovation to target the four levels at the same time, i.e. to *design for scapes*.

Design for scapes attains at two different modes of design:

(1) to act simultaneously in niches and regimes for a synergic value creation of users, organisations and ecosystems;
(2) to act with the precise intention to develop solutions responding to societal challenges, by developing and targeting the embedment of new values, this intentionality being included in several definitions of design-related concepts like the "transition design" one by Carnegie Mellon (2015).

The first mode just focuses the attention on the simultaneousness of the design action and orientation to the different levels of socio-technical systems, which has been discussed above.

The second is pivoted on the activation of mediation and negotiation mechanisms with regards to values. This second mode asks for a more strategic goal for design, i.e. conceiving the value creation dynamics and processes as functional to larger, global scale behavioural changes (activated by value creation), able to embed new values into a society.

Small-scale and locally anchored innovation projects can be carried out by individuals or groups and their capacity to look at things from a critical perspective, to frame problems and imagine solutions (diffuse design). At this level, they select and aggregate resources in light of their wishes and needs and value emerges from their situated actions in the context of use.

As we have already discussed, expert design can bring innovation a few steps forward. Expert design can create infrastructures by pre-aggregating resources that come already structured in the form of products and/or services and, as such, it deploys resources that can be re-adapted, appropriated and tailored by individuals and groups. Innovation projects need design competences for a wider impact of the innovation itself, since design abilities are effective in reducing the gap between the development and the adoption of a solution by targeting the value creation process.

Design for scapes pushes the discussion further, by suggesting a new conceptual framework to innovation: the scaling up of innovation is functional to the embedment of new values in the socio-technical context, the "global why" becomes relevant. When operating in the *design for scapes* mode a systemic, paradigmatic perspective is introduced to bring the innovation to respond to signals transmitted by the scape through an intentional guide of the value creation process.

Design for scapes embraces a multi-level perspective and addresses shifts in dimension and scale and aims for an expanded long-lasting impact of the design action across wider contexts of application in response to global societal challenges. *Design for scapes* asks for 'a new, expanded way of designing that is orientated by better future images and back casting, and that looks to cultivate niches that can challenge regimes' (Mulder and Loorbach 2016). Opening up to scape perspectives, design actions need a comprehensive approach that allows systematic and strategic experimentation with new ways of thinking, organising, and working in and with design. The diffusion of value creation across the various dimensions of scale in socio-technical systems needs the joint forces of transdisciplinary groups of experts and diffuse design.

Finally, the term *design for scapes* refers to those design interventions which aim at contributing to both situated and limited problem spheres, to broader phenomena of innovation, which configure large transitions of societies, urban environments and political governances: 'design for scapes' represents the whole set of design activities oriented to guarantee a dialogue between niches and regime within the framework of the different change processes activated by scape crises,[2] i.e. targeting global challenges which are embedded in such crises.

Furthermore, when considering the shifts in dimension and scale of *design for scapes*, a broader outlook is needed to consider the systemic implications of design actions. Design actions are seen as strictly interlinked to wider organisational, social, cultural and economic dimensions. Design artefacts are complex socio-technical systems which are affected by the interplay of multiple stakeholders —possibly with their own needs and wants. At this level, design thinking is much more concerned about bigger pictures, about complexity and uncertainty, about what Dan Hill identifies as the dark matter of design—the context, the organisational culture, policy environments, market mechanisms, legislation, finance models and other incentives, governance structures, tradition and habits, local culture and national identity, the habitats, situations and events that influence the design process (Hill 2012).

---

[2]See the discussion in Sect. 3.2.1.

Design for scapes raises innovative initiatives out of the scale of small changes within defined niches to the scale of socio-technical regimes (Geels and Schot 2007) in coherence with the needs of systemic changes; it also implies a change in practices, norms and routines, which makes the institutional frame for value co-creation processes (Vargo and Lusch 2015).

References

Bánáthy BH (1996) Designing social systems in a changing world. Plenum, NY
Björgvinsson E, Ehn P, Hillgren PA (2010) Participatory design and "democratizing innovation". PDC 2010, Sydney, Australia
Björgvinsson E, Ehn P, Per-Anders H (2012) Design things and design thinking: contemporary participatory design challenges. Des Issues 28(3):101–116
Binder T, de Michelis G, Ehn P, Jacucci G, Linde P, Wagner I (2011) Design things. The MIT Press, Cambridge
Carnegie Mellon School of Design (2015). Transition design 2015. https://design.cmu.edu/sites/default/files/Transition_Design_Monograph_final.pdf. Accessed Dec 2017
Castells M (ed) (2017) Another economy is possible: culture and economy in a time of crisis. Cambridge, Polity
Castells M et al (2017) Another economy is possible: culture and economy in a time of crisis. Polity Press, Cambridge
Chesbrough HW (2003) Open innovation: the new imperative for creating and profiting from technology. Harvard Business Press
Chesbrough HW (2007) Business model innovation: it's not just about technology anymore. Strategy Leadersh 35(6):12–17
Cross N (2011) Design thinking. Understanding how designers think and work. Bloomsbury Publishing, London
den Ouden E (2012) Innovation design. Creating value for people, organisations and society. Springer, London
Dvir R, Pasher E (2004) Innovation engines for knowledge cities: an innovation ecology perspective. J Knowl Manag 8(5):16–27
Ehn P, Nilsson EM, Topgaard R (2014) Making futures: marginal notes on innovation, design, and democracy. MIT Press, Cambridge, MA and London
Geels FW, Schot J (2007) Typology of sociotechnical transition pathways. Res Policy 36:399–417
Grin J, Rotmans J, Schot J (2010) Transitions to sustainable development: new directions in the study of long term transformative change. Routledge, New York
Hill D (2012) Dark matter and Trojan horses. A strategic design vocabulary. Strelka Press
Karasti H (2014) Infrastructuring in participatory design. In: Participatory design conference, vol 14, pp 141–150, Windhoek, Namibia
Krippendorff K (2006) Semantic turn: new foundations for design. CRC Taylor and Francis, Boca Raton
Le Dantec CA, Di Salvo C (2013) Infrastructuring and the formation of publics in participatory design. Soc Stud Sci 43(2):241–264
Lukens J (2013) DIY infrastructure and the scope of design practice. Des Issues 29(3):14–27
Manzini E (2015) Design, when everybody designs. MIT Press, Cambridge, Massachusetts, London, England

Metcalf GS (2014) Social systems and design. Springer, Japan

Mulder I, Loorbach D (2016) Rethinking design: transition design as a critical perspective to embrace societal challenges. In: Position paper at transition design symposium 2016: can design catalyse the great transition? Dartington

Normann R, Ramirez R (1994) Designing interactive strategy. Wiley, Chichester

Hillgren PA, Seravalli A, Emilson A (2011) Prototyping and infrastructuring in design for social innovation. CoDesign 7(3–4):169–183

Hillgren PA, Linde P, Peterson B (2013) Matryoshka dolls and boundary infrastructuring. Navigating among innovation policies and practices. In: Proceedings of participatory innovation conference, pp 422–429. Lahti, Finland

Schön DA (1987) Educating the reflective practitioner. Jossey-Bass, San Francisco

Secomandi F, Snelders D (2011) The object of service design. Des Issues 27(3):20–34

Simeone L (2016) Design moves, translational processes and academic enterpreneurship. In: Design labs. Doctoral Dissertation, Malmo University, Sweeden

Simon H (1969–1982) The science of artificial. The MIT Press, Cambridge

Star SL, Bowker GC (2002) How to infrastructure. In: Lievrouw LA, Livingstone S (eds) Handbook of new media: social shaping and consequences of Icts, pp 151–162. SAGE Publications, London; Thousand Oaks; New Delhi

Star SL, Ruhleder K (1996) Steps toward an ecology of infrastructure: design and access for large information spaces. Inf Syst Res 7(1):111–134

Vargo SL, Lusch RF (2004) Evolving to a new dominant logic for marketing. J Market 68:1–17

Vargo SL, Lusch RF (2008) Service-dominant logic: continuing the evolution. J Acad Mark Sci 36:1–10

Vargo SL, Lusch RF (2015) Institutions and axioms: an extension and update of service-dominant logic. J Acad Mark Sci 44(5):20

Verganti R (2009) Design-driven innovation: changing the rules of competition by radically innovating what things mean. Harvard Business School Publishing, Boston

Open Access This chapter is licensed under the terms of the Creative Commons Attribution 4.0 International License (http://creativecommons.org/licenses/by/4.0/), which permits use, sharing, adaptation, distribution and reproduction in any medium or format, as long as you give appropriate credit to the original author(s) and the source, provide a link to the Creative Commons license and indicate if changes were made.

The images or other third party material in this chapter are included in the chapter's Creative Commons license, unless indicated otherwise in a credit line to the material. If material is not included in the chapter's Creative Commons license and your intended use is not permitted by statutory regulation or exceeds the permitted use, you will need to obtain permission directly from the copyright holder.

Chapter 5
Design Enabled Innovation in Urban Environments

Grazia Concilio, Joe Cullen and Ilaria Tosoni

5.1 Changes in and from Urban Environments

As already highlighted in previous chapters, changes taking place in socio-technical systems are described by several authors in different ways through different models. The model described by Grin et al. is strongly coherent with the cities as situated, space-based socio-technical systems and is focussed on the relation among three different components: niches, where innovation takes place for the most part of its maturity process; regimes, the framework of rules and resources that constrains the way things happen in the city; and finally (land)scape, the system of culture and values which produces regimes, the component which is the most stable, the slowest to change (Grin et al. 2010).

Within this change model, innovation needs niches as protected spaces to be conceived of and nurtured: niches can allow the needed freedom in terms of behaviours, non-hierarchical relations, rules bending, etc., which makes room for creativity/design to shape novelties. For the most part, innovation is produced in niches and from there it finds its way to the higher levels (incremental/disruptive changes towards regimes in the framework of the scape). Nevertheless, this is not the only trigger for change. More effective are turbulences or perturbations taking place at the level of scapes; they activate change dynamics and mechanisms which may or may not intercept innovation processes (in the niches) depending on their preparedness in relation to the specific change.[1] High disturbances (shocks, disruptive changes, etc.) can open new "windows of opportunities" for regimes to act

---

[1] A synthetic description of such dynamics is given in Chap. 3.

G. Concilio (✉) · I. Tosoni
Politecnico di Milano, Milan, Italy
e-mail: grazia.concilio@polimi.it

J. Cullen
The Tavistock Institute, London, UK

on the innovation processes in the niches with a higher intensity (Grin et al. 2010). These last dynamics are, according to den Ouden (2012) more effective as these are already coherent with the transformation economy she envisages: following, in fact, changes coming from the scapes, these dynamics have global challenges embedded in their substance and sooner or later affect all the scales of socio-technical systems.

However, in both dynamics, niches play a relevant role. It is actually within niches that innovation is mainly developed and it is within niches that any change, starting from the scapes, lands and activates processes of embedding change into specific contexts. The dynamics of embedding change (called transitions by Grin et al. 2010) are co-evolution processes involving novelties development, their use and adoption, and the adaptation and adjustment of their institutional, organisational, regulative, praxis contexts (Grin et al. 2010: 11). Using the similitude between urban and biological systems it is clear that such a co-evolution implies a mutual selection among more diverse evolving populations (the niches) slowly producing irreversible patterns of change (Perez 1983; Nelson 1994; Oudshoorn and Pinch 2003; Kemp et al. 2007).

In the networked nature of cognitive, economic and practical interactions inside the urban environments and in inter-urban systems up to the global scale, processes of embedding innovation assume a rhizome-like nature (Castells 2012). A rhizome is a stem of a plant (usually underground) often sending out roots and shoots from its nodes. Rhizomes develop from axillary buds. The rhizome also retains the ability to allow new shoots to grow upwards. If a rhizome is separated each piece may be able to give rise to a new plant. Similarly, innovation does not start and end up in the same place, in the same city. Throughout its maturity process, it moves and intercepts other more or less similar systems (contexts), it creates new nodes (nodes are portions of the rhizome-like system, separated from the others, but all together contributing to the system's growth, i.e. to the change) where new shots are created. Every time an innovation process enters a new city or a new portion of the same city, a new node is created, autonomous from the rest; a new innovation story, a new plant, starts giving rise to another plant, a new node of the same innovation movement contributing to the change. Each new story, each new plant is not exactly the same: each adapts to the local, contextual conditions (a dialogue between niches and specific regime is started), slowly giving rise to a complex movement made out of different interpretations and characterisations of the way a specific innovation interacts with the urban networks, in the urban networks. Places count, local conditions count; cities, as network hubs (Gutzmer 2016) count in the embedment processes.

Managing change embedment dynamics means considering, among other aspects, learning as a co-evolving facet in a cyclical and iterative process (Grin et al. 2010; Kemp et al. 2007). Learning, in urban systems, is spatialised: the spaces through which knowledge moves are not simply landscapes of learning, but constitutive of it. In urban spaces, it operates as the 'education of attention' (Gibson, Rader 1979; Ingold 2000), the socio-political rooting of new values (activated by the large scale creation of new value meanings and functions) produced by innovation. This means that learning entails shifts in ways of seeing, where 'ways of seeing' are defined not simply as an optical activity, but as intensive, haptic immersion based on translation, coordination and dwelling (McFarlane 2011).

Translation refers to the distribution and adoption of knowledge, ideas, and resources across multiple dimensions, from activists sharing ideas to planners and policy makers learning from different cities and contexts. The translation concept challenges the diffusion model that traces movement as innovation (Latour 1986, 1999). While the diffusion model focuses on travel as the product of the action of an authoritative centre transmitting knowledge, translation focuses on travel as the product of what different actors do in and through distributions with objects (statements, orders, artefacts, products, goods, etc.) (Gherardi and Nicolini 2000: p. 335). That is, translation emphasises the spatialities through which knowledge moves and seeks to unpack how they make a difference, whether through hindering, facilitating, amplifying, distorting, contesting or radically repackaging knowledge. This draws attention to the importance of various forms of intermediaries, and promotes two inseparable relational perspectives: first, the importance of relationships between the 'near' and 'far' in producing knowledge, for instance in the ways in which the internet or a policy exchange may bring distant actors closer; and second, the agency capacities of materials in producing knowledge and learning, for example the differential and contingent role of urban plans, documents, maps, databases or models in producing, shaping and contesting urban learning (Amin and Cohendet 2004). Translation positions learning as a constitutive act of world-making (embedding), rather than occurring prior to or following from engagement with the world; the travelling act here is not a mere supplement to learning, but constitutive of it; and determines the way innovation enters, embeds itself and propagates throughout the urban networks.

Coordination takes into account the fact that learning depends on constantly constructing relational systems between different domains through domain networks. The transition along the innovation process, throughout the development of its maturity levels, is not linear and coordination allows the interactions between the three structural systems: innovation niches, regimes, and the scape. The more developed the maturity level of innovation is, the more higher structures (regimes and less so the scape) are affected; they enter what Varvarousis and Callis (quoted in Castells 2017) call "liminal conditions" (2017, p. 131), i.e conditions in which they are unstable with respect to their previous state, identity, while they still have to conquer, consolidate a new one. These liminal conditions characterise those spheres of practices which are undergoing a change process and can be coherently associated with a new one, the seed of innovation, the transformative potentials. In these liminal conditions institutions are ephemeral; they emerge and perish while decentralising-recentralising. In liminal conditions, coordination frames learning as the complex self-definition of urban identity (Guntzmer 2016) and as the output of both institutional/public decisions and investments, and diffuse transformation activities and initiatives of the city. Both of these self-definition modes are concrete and clear consequences (the firsts in coherence, the second often in conflict/contrast response) of urban public visions and goals and are possible intakes for innovation actors to plague in the urban dynamics and to become key actors of the self-definition mechanisms.

The self-definition mechanisms of a city have the potential to create multiple levels of information possibly feeding innovation strategies.

Dwelling refers to how learning is lived, and how over time people tune and modify their behaviours. Quoting Ingold (2000), McFarlane (2011) looks at learning in relation to dwelling, i.e. the way knowledge is developed and internalized (quoting Nonaka and Takeuchi 1995) through a process of immersion in their lived-in environments' (Ingold 2000: 154, 168, quoted in McFarlane 2011). Dwelling implies the creation of conditions for knowledge to unconsciously feed a practical ability, notice and respond to changing contexts. While dwelling people develop a new way to perceive the world and to contribute to world-making. Dwelling is what brings knowledge into a complete correspondence with action: knowledge and action, according to Zeleny (2010), correspond when people have experienced and experimented on it in real life and have transformed it from an information-like use to a 'way of seeing' through the "education of attention'. Relevant to our discussion is that dwelling represents the process in which values can be revised as an output (a possible one) of the value creation in an innovation process: dwelling allows the experimentation of values through practical engagement in real life. It represents the highest strategical opportunity for embedding innovation in response to the challenges which originate in the scape.

What emerges, then, is a view of the city as a multiple learning machine based on three interrelated ongoing processes: translation, or the relational distributions through which learning is produced as a socio-material epistemology of displacement and change; coordination, or the construction of functional systems that enable learning as a means of coping with complexity and facilitating adaptation; and dwelling, or the education of attention through which learning operates as a way of seeing and inhabiting urban worlds (McFarlane 2011).

Knowledge is more complex than information and includes tacit elements (Polanyi 1966). Important elements of knowledge are embodied in the minds and bodies of agents, in the routines of firms and, not least of all, in the relationships between people and organisations. This makes knowledge, and therefore learning, spatially sticky and embedded in relationships and interactions between people and organisations, i.e. embedded in the networks. Looking at cities as network hubs means for innovation and Design Enabled Innovation to use relationships as carriers of knowledge and interactions thus making embedment a process by which new knowledge is produced and learned (Johnson 2008). Cities have the capacity to act as "densifiers and enrichers" of the knowledge that is there; they make it easier for the knowledge to be shared as they connect different knowledge bases and different learning processes (Gutzmer 2016).

Urban learning is the backbone of innovation when contributing to change processes. It is the engine of the rhizome-like dynamics when playing within urban environments and acting from its inside out. Learning, in fact, enables the understanding of, and the plugging into the context for new nodes and shoots of the rhizome-like innovation system and for the development of a reciprocating interaction with urban networks. It is, in the end, the way innovation ignites, at the very beginning of the maturity process, in one specific urban environment by contributing to, or being inspired by, the *idearium* and by, in the same system or in (several) others, experimenting in the *problems-labs*. It is the way in which innovation development is carried out by exploring and using the (urban) *resource pot* and by positioning itself in the *market*. It is the way transition in regime is activated by *political arena*. This learning is spatialised with regards to the embedding of innovation in global realms thus contributing to change processes.

5.2 The Urban/Design Interplay Towards Innovation

The different dynamics described above do not take place in the same (urban) context. Urban environments are open and networked by nature (Castells 1996, 1997, 1998) and any change or innovation is a complex process of learning (knowledge use and production) inside a complex system of diverse networks while having cities as entry and exit points. Recapping from the previous chapters:

(1) In Chap. 2 we summarised the changes pathways described by Grin et al. (2010) and mapped them onto the innovation maturity levels (see Fig. 5.1);

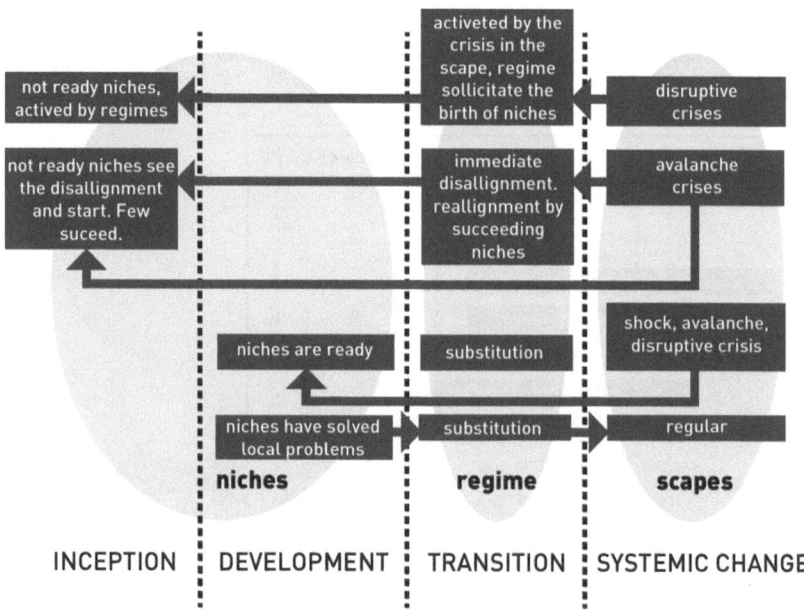

Fig. 5.1 Transitions and innovation maturity (adapted from Geels 2005, as in Grin et al. 2010)

(2) in Chap. 3 we described the interaction between cities and innovation through five main dimensions/interfaces: resource pot, problems lab, idearium, political arena, and market; the first three are more active and effective at the early maturity stage of innovation (inception and development) and mainly relate to niches; the last two have their prevailing role in the interaction with innovation processes at their late stage (development and transition) and mainly relate to regime (see Fig. 5.2);
(3) in Chap. 4 we described the role of design within the change pathways and in relation to each component of socio-technical systems; here we summarise that discussion through Table 5.1; in this table expert and diffuse design are not distinguished and a general role is assigned to design.

We have developed the previous chapters to highlight the deep interconnection among cities, innovation and design through change dynamics. This interconnection is represented by the two figures and the table provided above. From now on we will take this exploration to an increasingly in-depth analysis.

Change dynamics taking places in niches (when innovation maturity moves from inception to development) are explained by the 3D innovation model described in this chapter. In niches, design activates value production and by doing this it starts the embedment of innovation into one or more contexts. When such contexts are urban environments, the embedment process is accompanied by the five mechanisms described in 3.2.1. This embedding can become intense up to the point that it exits the protected environment of the niches and starts dialoguing with the regimes. The deeper the embedment the more mature the innovation becomes.

An explicative example of such a dynamic is the way in which cities have embedded the epiphanies of changes represented by guerrilla gardening initiatives

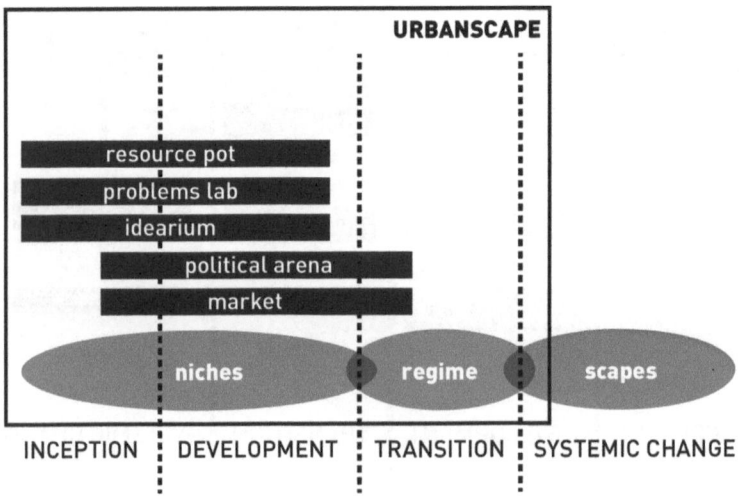

Fig. 5.2 Innovation in urban environments

Table 5.1 The role of design in transition pathways

Design and transition pathways		Roles of design	
	Scape	Regimes	Niches
Transformation pathway	Disruptive change	Provides interpretative framework of the crisis Creates the vision in relation to the regime problems and instruments	Provides interpretative framework of the crises in relation to practices Translates the vision into solutions
De-alignement and re-alignment pathway	Avalanche change	Provides interpretative framework of the crisis Creates the vision in relation to the regime problems and instruments	Provides interpretative framework of the crises in relation to practices Generates visions Produces solution and supports their transition towards the regime
Technological substitution pathway	Specific shock Avalanche change Disruptive change		Senses the incumbent crisis Generates visions Produces solution and supports their positioning as alternatives to the regime
Reconfiguration pathways		Creates the conditions for the embedment of niche-innovations in relation to the regime problems and instruments	Senses local problems Works on local practices Supports the embedment of innovations in the regime

taking places in many different cities all over the world and then have transformed them into more and more mature initiatives towards the so called "public contracts for the management of the commons".

The maturity process mapped in the 3D model above is the result of the interaction between the innovation process and its urban environment. In Fig. 5.3 the interaction of each innovation step and the urban environment is described as per the roles played by different urban interfaces.

The selected example does not represent the entire maturity process: it takes into account the most relevant progressions of this innovation but, for example, does not include the initial resistances and obstacles created by regime to illegal modes of transforming public spaces as is the case for guerrilla gardeners. What is important here is to put in evidence that, throughout the innovation maturity process, the interaction with the urban interfaces is a complex negotiation dialogue exclusively possible through design (Fig. 5.4).

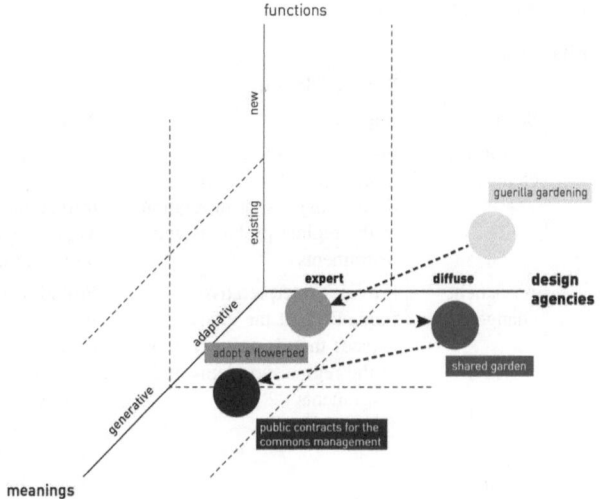

Fig. 5.3 From guerrilla gardening to contracts for common goods: the innovation maturity process in the niche towards a regime

Cities are multidimensional entities with many contradicting operators and potential innovation forces. Relevant for innovation to harness the available potential is the ability to activate new connections with such forces while disconnecting others, i.e. to activate new modes for knowledge and value creation through the interaction with the provided interfaces. It is through these dynamics that design can best play out its enabling role in innovation processes (Table 5.2).

Design can be seen as a social integrator (see the discussion carried out by Gutzmer 2016 interpreting Latour's idea of design), as the enabler of the dynamics depicted above within a single urban environment or enabling the transfer among diverse urban environments, i.e. acting at different levels of the complex network. Design and the use of design outputs such as artifacts, sketches, visual representations or prototypes (Simeone et al. 2017) enable solutions to be embedded (at any innovation maturity stage) within specific urban contexts and is able to develop and work with them in order for them to be relevant in other contexts. This embedding represents a (design) process in between meanings and functions (see the 3D model), which shapes value by infrastructuring practices in real life, which are targeted by the innovation process:

- adaptation of the interplay between meanings and functions which the solution brings with itself form another urban context;
- creation of new meanings through functions in order to plug into the urban contexts;

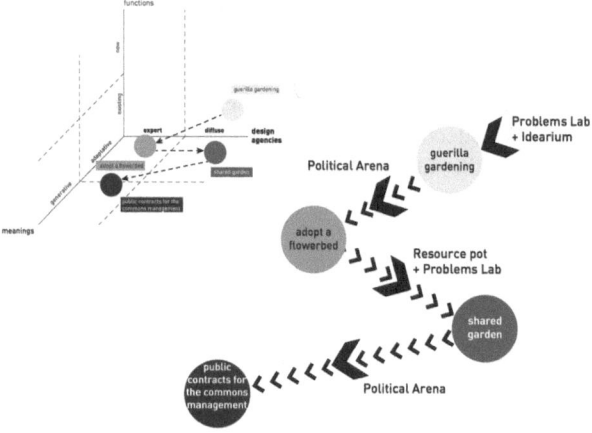

Fig. 5.4 The role of urban-innovation interfaces in the change from guerrilla gardening to contracts for common goods

Table 5.2 Design fields mapped onto cities-innovation interfaces

Cities-innovation interfaces	Design fields
Resource pot	Co-design Networking
Problems lab	Experiments design Participatory Design Prototyping
Idearium	Idea generation Idea incremental development
Political arena	Policy design Interaction design
Market	Business design Marketing Communication design

- ideation of new functions for the sake of developing or empowering new meanings;
- reinforcing and enriching meanings in order to support the maturing of innovation in the transition between niches and regimes.

In both cases, either change starts in/by niches or by turbulence in scapes, the role of design, is that of sensing the potentials of change and translating it into a vision able to guide the innovative action at both the regimes and niches levels.

The city is the sphere in which most of the social and cultural productivity factors at play become active thus feeding and intensifying the learning processes described in paragraph 6.1. Such learning processes, possible at such intensity only in rich, complex and networked environments as cities are, create reciprocal benefits among cities and design. The former appear more obvious, and are still very important; the latter are not yet well discussed in literature but relevant in the economy of our discussion.

For urban environments, design can be considered as a driver, a trigger for the creation of urban knowledge spill-over processes, encouraging and nourishing the creation of networked collective knowledge. The knowledge created in the cities is inherently connected to the notion of new and of innovation, since such knowledge production is nurtured by, and nurtures, the networks which cities belong to and act in (Gutzmer 2016).

Also, for urban environments, design, particularly design approaches for scapes, represents a strategic resource for accelerating change processes (in the simultaneous work in niches and regimes) by more effectively and more rapidly experimenting with responses to global challenges which are stressing them more and more. Design, in fact, is not a simple methodology for creative value production, but a skill to enable action through a comprehensive approach. It is hence needed to monitor changes in the specific contexts (spatial, institutional, socio-technical…) by exploiting the "cracks" in the systems as a lever to increase the amplitude of the innovation transformative potential.

Finally, in urban environments design objects are not only part of spatial performative constitutions of reality; design objects integrate, and are part of, the social and cultural environments that the city is made up of. Design objects can be conceived as connectors to this environment. The connective role is not something that simply happens; it can, and arguably has to, be fostered through the process of designing the objects (Gutzmer 2016: 34–35).

For design, urban environments represent a rich opportunity for different reasons. Potential for change is not revealed in an undifferentiated manner: cities are the most important sensors of these changes as they are the hubs among which several diverse networks interweave; cities are the main responsible environments of problems and shocks activating signals from the scapes, so they represent the best environments for design to sense changes and start innovation in a competitive time frame.

Furthermore, design, as a basic means of social production, is also a way to interpret contemporary cultural productivity. Considering the networked nature of the city, cultural forms and social modes of mutual understanding and visibility are created by processes that can be described as design-intensive. The city is the play-ground of these design processes. It is in the urban environment that design objects develop their full cultural potential. The city provides a frame of reference for the language of design.

In addition, within urban environments, design can better learn about itself as to develop further its theoretical and methodological framework. The dwelling mechanism is a networked phenomenon: it is capable of embedding knowledge (and therefore values) into the urbanscape, however this is not only true for innovation products, it is true for the complex system of involved knowledge, and therefore also for design knowledge and practice. Dwelling relates to learning at any level of the involved networks and about any specific involved contents. Within the complex machine for learning, as is a city (McFarlane 2011), 'education to attention' also includes the modes of innovation thus making design an object of education and therefore scaling up its use, diffusion and embedment.

The urban is therefore productive of Design Enabled Innovation primarily in two ways: (1) the city guarantees the existence of conditions (normative, economic, cognitive, informational and networking) for the activation of Design Enabled Innovation processes; but also (2) the city inspires ideas because it is the city that faces most of today's global challenges. Urban problems and challenges tend to nest in the *complexity zone* (Stacey 2002) therefore they call for creative solutions developed through erratic (less structured, open, ...) decision making. These creative processes dialogue with complexity generating innovative solutions to urban problems.

5.3 Sensing the Innovation Capacity of Cities

Although the statistical evidence reported confirms the convergence of demographic and innovation trends in the metropolitan areas of Europe, cities obviously differ from one another in being more or less effective systems for innovation generation. Effectiveness means that a city is able to create, preserve and broaden the conditions for innovation potential to become productive of value.

The book *Innovative Cities* edited by Simmie (2001) proved that cities contribute to innovation in two different ways: with their size per se (relevant as it matters in terms of the richness and variety of the external, facilitating factors to innovation which firms may draw on) and with the economic and political power relations which are associated with the number and ranking of their firms and decision-making institutions (institutional arrangements external to firms). Stuttgart, Milan and Amsterdam were described there in terms of their innovation generation capacity and, quite naturally, no single interpretation was developed that could explain the different attitudes and abilities of those cities to drive and host innovation. The book, however, confirmed the relevance of two assets which are widely shared by the literature (highly qualified and knowledgeable labour, fixed capital infrastructures and communication hubs) and identified a few additional contributing factors:

(1) The longer cities have successfully experienced innovation, the more effectively they are capable of driving and hosting it;
(2) The stronger the national/regional performance in terms of innovation, the higher cities are positioned in the national/regional rankings, the more urban environments can facilitate innovation within the firms located therein;
(3) Knowledge assets are not only relevant within a city, but also in relation to its international connections (with customers, other businesses...) and their time proximity;

(4) A city's ability to deal with changing circumstances and to re-invent itself, practised for centuries, is one of the keys to their relative success in the twenty-first century.

In addition to the above, other sources of cities' innovation generation capacities may be rooted in:

- the existence of specific strategies for activating or hosting Design Enabled Innovation (Verilhac 2011);
- the cities being prone to develop, prototype, experiment, test and evaluate novel innovation opportunities (Karvonen and van Heur 2014), i.e. open to learning;
- the richness of urban interactions among users, designers, researchers and companies (Foss et al. 2011);
- the way cities govern the networked dynamics of organisations and therefore organisational flexibility (Roper and Love 2005);
- their capability to support the creation of public places where innovative solutions to public problems are developed through the creation of networks, partnerships and events, thus providing environments where people can exchange new ideas, do business or trade, or simply enjoy the evening in offices, restaurants, theatres, streets, public parks, or squares (Manzini and Staszowski 2013; Manzini 2015; Gehl 2011);
- the emergence of creative communities, who co-design and incubate socially innovative initiatives (Meroni 2008).

On his part, Hawkes (2001) identifies culture as the fourth pillar of sustainable development, together with Society, the economy and the environment. In this way, the definition of development gains a "cultural slant" (Project Sostenuto 2012[2]). However, including culture in the innovation capacity of urban environments also implies narrowing the focus on the dimension of cultural creativity—often expressed in forms of diffused design initiatives (Manzini 2015)—since, as the Council of Europe itself recognises, culture and creativity are closely interwoven. Creativity is also at the very heart of innovation—defined as the successful exploitation of new ideas, concepts, expressions and models through developing new products, services, processes, businesses, organisational settings, industrial and aesthetic designs and ultimately the establishment of alternative ways of responding to societal needs, which can also improve the performance and efficiency of public and private organisations. Therefore, creativity is paramount in order to foster the innovation capacity of urban stakeholders (citizens and civil servants, public and private actors, profit and not for profit organisations, etc.).

However, despite several suggestions (some discussed in the Introduction to this book) to align the concept of innovation capacity of cities to the growing need for responses to global challenges, it is quite clear that the prevailing definition of innovation still belongs to an 'instrumental' paradigm. This considers innovation—

---

[2]Sostenuto project (2012) Culture as a Factor for Economic and Social Innovation. University of Valencia.

and therefore innovation capacity—in relation to the contribution it can make to supporting traditional (i.e. market-based and profit-driven or utility-oriented) production and consumption models. Thus, most of the work on measuring and sensing capacity for innovation has been polarised towards two extremes—either the country level, with the large scale and standardised surveys such as the CIS presented above, methodologically grounded in the Frascati Manual (OECD 1981) or the Oslo Manual (OECD 1992); or, using psychometric and behavioural measures, at the level of individual decision makers within organisations (Forsman 2011). Likewise, as documented in the previous section, most approaches to innovation capacity measurement focus on 'science' and 'technology', instead of other 'creative' forms of human ingenuity, although there have been more recent attempts to measure non-R&D based innovation activities like those performed by poets, novelists, artists, entertainers, actors, designers and architects (Florida 2005).

The fundamental problem with traditional measures of innovation capacity is that they are based on old and outdated understandings of what growth and innovation is about. These understandings are in deep crisis today. In a lecture to launch the UK Royal Society's 'Changing Minds' program, the RSA's Chief Executive, Matthew Taylor, suggested that the current crisis of Western societies reflects a deep cultural inertia, and an inability to move beyond comfortable, although outdated, notions of how humans think and learn. Our common understanding of innovation is rooted in an idea of 'selfhood' that is increasingly being questioned, and which cannot easily deal with the huge challenges created by the 'progress' of humankind. The wicked problems of climate change, ageing population, pressure on welfare budgets, mass migration, growing disillusion with established democratic institutions have led to an increasing conviction that the conventions which have shaped our understanding of growth and innovation are no longer fit for their purpose.[3] This has led to calls for action, even by the EU Institutions, targeting the construction of new frameworks to support 'socio-ecological transitions' for a new sustainable Europe (COM 2011/0808).

Against this background, organisations like OECD have begun to re-think their positions on what innovation is and what it needs to do. A recent publication on assessing the innovation capacity of cities and urban regions presents a radically new perspective. Instead of focusing on 'capacity', the OECD focuses on 'resilience'. Pointing out that large urban systems are particularly vulnerable to foreseen and unforeseen threats—such as structural industrial changes (e.g. relocations or closures of a city's key firms); economic emergencies (e.g. the global financial turmoil of 2007/08 and the resulting, diffused sovereign debt crises); massive population inflows/outflows; natural disasters (such as earthquakes, floods and hurricanes); disruptions of the energy supplies; and huge political attacks against consolidated leaderships—the OECD concentrates on the cities' resilience to such shocks and stresses. In this perspective, innovative potential is re-packaged as 'resilience'—the ability to "absorb, adapt, transform and prepare for past and

---

[3]RSA Changing Minds: preparing for an era of neurological reflexivity, 30th June 2008.

future shocks and stresses in order to ensure sustainable development, well-being and inclusive growth" (Sugahara and Bermont (2016) OECD).

Following this new 'resilience' framework, Table 5.3 lists a set of criteria/indicators which might be considered and applied in order to sense innovation potential within cities.

Although the OECD's 'resilience' concept represents a first move away from conventional notions of innovation, the latter still dominate the field. For example, as will be described in the Chap. 3, the standard narrative on Design Enabled Innovation is still based on a 'functional' perspective. A similar functional framework for sensing, identifying and assessing urban innovation would then be based on the technical, institutional, economic, and structural characteristics of innovation and focus on attributes like:

- organisational/partnership structures
- adaptive design thinking
- citizen empowerment
- bridging of professional and political divides

Table 5.3 Urban innovation capacity criteria/indicators (based on OECD 'Resilience' framework)

Criteria/indicator	Characteristics
Adaptiveness	An adaptive urban system manages uncertainty by evolving—modifying standards, norms or past behaviour—using evidence to identify solutions and applying the knowledge gained from past experience when making decisions about the future
Robustness	A robust urban system can absorb shocks and emerge without significant losses to its functionality. Robustness depends on a system which is well-designed, built and managed to absorb the impact of a shock and continue to operate
Redundancy	Redundant urban systems are able to meet the need for spare capacity when faced with unexpected demand, a disruptive event or extreme pressure. This entails intentionally developing or having access to more than one source of action, service or service provider when necessary
Flexibility	A flexible urban system allows individuals, households, businesses, communities and government to adjust behaviour or actions in order to rapidly respond to change
Resourcefulness	A resourceful urban system can effectively and quickly restore the functionality of essential services and systems in a crisis or under highly constrained conditions, with the resources available
Inclusivity	An inclusive urban system ensures that diverse actors and communities are fully consulted, engaged and empowered in the policy process, including in the policy design stage when possible
Integration	An integrated urban system promotes a co-operative and, ideally, collaborative or participatory approach to policy making and programming that transcends sectoral and administrative boundaries to better ensure coherent decisions and effective investment

- adaptability to change and resilience
- recognition of sense of place and context
- integration of design and economic development
- capacity to access international networks of knowledge and innovation
- capacity to anchor external knowledge from people, institutions and firms
- capacity to diffuse new innovation and knowledge in the wider economy
- knowledge creation
- knowledge exploitation.

Design is explicitly referred to in this attribute list. Sensing the performance of a city in its regard, as for any other attribute listed above, remains a complex work, which needs to be carried out in balance between qualitative and quantitative indicators.[4]

References

Amin A, Cohendet P (2004) Architectures of knowledge: firms, capabilities, and communities. Oxford University Press

Castells M (1996) The information age: economy, society, and culture, vol I. The Rise of the Network Society, Blackwell

Castells M (1997) The information age: economy, society and culture, vol. 2. The power of identity, Blackwell

Castells M (1998) The information age: economy, society and culture, vol. 3. End of millennium, Blackwell Publishing, Oxford

Castells M (2012) Networks of outrage and hope – social movements in the Internet age, Chichester, UK, Wiley

Castells M (ed) (2017) Another economy is possible: culture and economy in a time of crisis. Cambridge, Polity

den Ouden E (2012) Innovation design. Creating value for people, organisations and society. Springer-Verlag, London

Foss NJ, Laursen K, Pedersen T (2011) Linking customer interaction and innovation: the mediating role of new organizational practices. Organ Sci 22(4):980–999

Forsman H (2011) Innovation capacity and innovation development in small enterprises. A comparison between the manufacturing and service sectors. Res Policy 40(5):739–750

Gehl J (2011) Life between buildings: using public space. Island Press

Gherardi S, Nicolini D (2000) To transfer is to transform: the circulation of safety knowledge. Organization 7(2):329–348

Gibson E, Rader N (1979) Attention. In: Hale GA, Lewis M (eds) Attention and cognitive development. Springer, Boston, MA

Grin J, Rotmans J, Schot J (2010) Transitions to sustainable development: new directions in the study of long term transformative change. Routledge, New York

Gutzmer A (2016) Urban innovation networks, understanding the city as a strategic resource. Springer International Publishing Switzerland

Hawkes J (2001) The fourth pillar of sustainability: culture's essential role in public planning. Common Ground

---

[4]See https://composite-indicators.jrc.ec.europa.eu/cultural-creative-cities-monitor/#, the Cultural and Creative Cities Monitor, for an attempt in this respect.

Ingold T (2000) The perception of the environment: essays on livelihood, Dwelling and Skill. Routledge, London

Johnson B (2008) Cities, systems of innovation and economic development. In: Innovation. Manag Policy Pract 10(2–3):146–155

Karvonen A, van Heur B (2014) Urban laboratories: experiments in reworking cities. In: Int J Urban Reg Res 38(2):379–392

Kemp R, Loorbach D, Rotmans J (2007) Transition management as a model for managing processes of co-evolution towards sustainable development. Int J Sustain Dev World Ecol 14 (1):78–91. https://doi.org/10.1080/13504500709469709

Latour B (1986) Visualisation and cognition: drawing things together. In: Kuklick H (ed) Knowledge and society studies in the sociology of culture past and present, vol 6. Jai Press, pp 1–40

Latour B (1999) Pandora's hope: essays on the reality of science studies. Harvard University Press, Cambridge

Manzini E, Staszowski (2013) Public and collaborative: exploring the intersection of design, social innovation and public policy. epub, DESIS Network. http://nyc.pubcollab.org/files/DESIS_PandC_Book.pdf

Manzini E (2015) Design, when everybody designs. MIT Press, Cambridge, Massachusetts, London, England

McFarlane C (2011) The city as a machine for learning. Trans Insts Br Geogr 36:360–376. https://doi.org/10.1111/j.1475-5661.2011.00430.x

Meroni A (2008) Strategic design: where are we now? Reflection around the foundations of a recent discipline. Strateg Des Res J 1(1):31–38

Nelson RR (1994) Economic growth via the coevolution of technology and institutions. Leydesdorff & Van den Besselaar, pp 21–32

Nonaka I, Takeuchi H (1995) The knowledge creating company. Oxford University Press

OECD (1981) The measurement of scientific and technical activities: Frascati Manual. Paris

OECD (1992) Oslo manual: the measurement of scientific and technological activities: proposed guidelines for collecting and interpreting technological innovation data. Paris

Oudshoorn NEJ, Pinch T (2003) How users matter: the co-construction of users and technologies. MIT Press, Cambridge, MA

Polanyi M (1966) The logic of tacit inference. Philosophy 41(155):1–18

Perez C (1983) Structural change and the assimilation of new technologies in the economic and social system. Futures 15(4):357–375

Roper S, Love JH (2005) Innovation success and business performance—an All-Island Analysis. All island business model research report. InterTradeIreland, July 2005

Simeone L, Secundo G, Schiuma G (2017) Knowledge translation mechanisms in open innovation: the role of design in R&D projects. J Knowl Manag 21(6):1406–1429

Simmie J (2001) Innovative cities. Taylor & Francis

Sugahara M, Bermont L (2016) Energy and resilient cities. In: OECD regional development working papers, No. 2016/05. OECD Publishing, Paris

Verilhac I (2011) LUPI Innovative uses and practices lab. In: 17th international conference core of the design creative city living lab, presented at the concurrent enterprising (ICE), p 17

Zeleny M (2010) Knowledge of enterprise: knowledge management or knowledge technology? Governing and Managing Knowledge in Asia: 2nd, pp 23–57

Open Access This chapter is licensed under the terms of the Creative Commons Attribution 4.0 International License (http://creativecommons.org/licenses/by/4.0/), which permits use, sharing, adaptation, distribution and reproduction in any medium or format, as long as you give appropriate credit to the original author(s) and the source, provide a link to the Creative Commons license and indicate if changes were made.

The images or other third party material in this chapter are included in the chapter's Creative Commons license, unless indicated otherwise in a credit line to the material. If material is not included in the chapter's Creative Commons license and your intended use is not permitted by statutory regulation or exceeds the permitted use, you will need to obtain permission directly from the copyright holder.